CONTENTS

ONLINE ACTIVITIES

On some of the pages you will see QR codes. These QR codes take you to online Purple Mash activities which support learning from the relevant page.

To use the QR codes, scan the QR code with the camera on your web enabled tablet, click on the link and the activity will appear on screen.

Alternatively, QR readers are available on the app store for your device.

SCAN CODE

purple mash

□ - with online activity

Published 2025. Little Brother Books Ltd, Ground Floor, 23 Southernhay East, Exeter, Devon EX1 1QL
books@littlebrotherbooks.co.uk | www.littlebrotherbooks.co.uk
Printed in the United Kingdom.
Little Brother Books, 77 Camden Street Lower, Dublin D02 XE80.

NUMBERS TO 10,000,000

Wallace has a new invention: the Mega-Number Cruncher 9000, a gadget that counts cheese portions up to 10,000,000! Wallace excitedly tests it, but can Gromit help him figure out if they really have that many cheese portions?

1

The machine has given the numbers of cheese portions in words. Write the numbers as digits.

Five million two hundred thirty-four thousand one hundred twenty-one — 5,234,121

a. Eight million six hundred seventy-five thousand four hundred three

b. Three million one hundred ninety-two thousand seven hundred eighty-four

c. Nine million forty-eight thousand two hundred sixty-five

d. Six million four hundred thirty-one thousand nine hundred

2

Look at each pair of numbers and write down the new number they make in digits.

a. 320,000 + 1,100,312 =

b. 250,000 + 2,200,450 =

c. 530,000 + 3,300,678 =

d. 140,000 + 4,400,890 =

e. 360,000 + 5,500,123 =

3

The Mega-Number Cruncher 9000 has counted the cheese portions and given the answer as:

7	3	4	5	2	1	0

Using this number, answer the questions below.

a. If there are 40,000 more cheese portions how many are there now?

b. If there are 100,000 less cheese portions how many are there now?

c. What is the value of the digit in the hundred thousands place?

d. If there are 300,000 more cheese portions how many are there now?

e. If there are 500,000 less cheese portions how many are there now?

ROUNDING NUMBERS

Gromit is in Wallace's workshop and has come across his plans to go to the moon. It says the moon is 384,402km away. Can you help Gromit figure out the rounded number?

If the key number is a 5 you need to round up. 55 rounded to the nearest 10 becomes 60. 1,579 rounded to the nearest 1,000 becomes 2,000.

1

The moon is 384,402km away.
Help Gromit round the distance in a range of ways.

a. Round to the nearest **10** = ______

b. Round to the nearest **100** = ______

c. Round to the nearest **1,000** = ______

d. Round to the nearest **10,000** = ______

e. Round to the nearest **100,000** = ______

2

Look at the questions below. Put a circle around the correct answer.

a. Round 47,834 to the nearest **10,000**	50,000	40,000	47,000
b. Round 89,462 to the nearest **1,000**	89,000	89,500	90,000
c. Round 23,679 to the nearest **100**	23,600	23,700	23,680
d. Round 12,345 to the nearest **10**	12,340	12,350	12,300
e. Round 65,432 to the nearest **100,000**	60,000	100,000	70,000

3

Gromit is helping Wallace organise the workshop and counting what they have in there. To keep things simple, he decides to round the numbers.

a. Gromit counts **23,489** bolts. What is this number rounded to the nearest **10,000?** ______

b. Wallace estimates **92,501** nuts. What is this number rounded to the nearest **1,000**? ______

c. Gromit finds **42,567** washers. What is this number rounded to the nearest **100**? ______

d. Wallace lists **11,132** screws. What is this number rounded to the nearest **10**? ______

e. Gromit calculates **55,423** springs. What is this number rounded to the nearest **100,000**? ______

PROBLEM SOLVING

Wendolene is expanding her wool shop and has received three large shipments of wool: 6,234,789 in one shipment, 4,567,123 in another, and 2,345,678 in a third. She needs help working with these large numbers through place value and rounding.

1

Answer these questions about the wool in Wendolene's shop.

a. What is the digit in the millions place of the number 6,234,789?

b. What is 4,567,123 rounded to the nearest 1,000,000?

c. How many hundred thousands are in the number 2,345,678?

d. What is 6,234,789 rounded to the nearest 1,000,000?

e. What is the value of the digit in the hundred thousands place of 4,567,123?

f. What is 2,345,678 rounded to the nearest 1,000,000?

g. What is the digit in the ten thousands place of 6,234,789?

h. What is 4,567,123 rounded to the nearest 100,000?

NEGATIVE NUMBERS

Wallace is using his new invention, the Snowmanotron, to build an amazing snow sculpture. Wallace shivers as the weather outside gets colder and the temperature drops by 10 degrees.

1

Work out the changing temperature.

a. -3°C - 6°C = ☐ °C

b. -8°C + 5°C = ☐ °C

c. -12°C - 4°C = ☐ °C

d. -5°C + 7°C = ☐ °C

e. -10°C - 3°C = ☐ °C

f. -15°C + 10°C = ☐ °C

g. -20°C - 5°C = ☐ °C

h. -6°C + 8°C = ☐ °C

i. -25°C - 10°C = ☐ °C

j. -18°C + 9°C = ☐ °C

2

Complete these number sequences.

a.	-10	-5		5		15
b.	20	15	10		0	
c.		-12	-9		-3	0
d.	5	1		-7		-15
e.	13	7		-5		-17

3

During the day, Wallace heads outside and then back inside to warm up. Answer the questions to calculate the new temperatures at various times of the day.

a. If the temperature at 8am is **-8°C** and it drops by **5°C**, what is the new temperature?

☐ °C

b. At 11am, the temperature is **-3°C**, but it warms up by **7°C**. What is the new temperature?

☐ °C

c. At 1pm, Wallace goes outside, and the temperature is **-15°C**. It then drops by another **10°C**. What is the temperature now?

☐ °C

d. By 3pm, the temperature is **-12°C**, but the winter sun raises it by **8°C**. What is the new temperature?

☐ °C

e. At the end of the day, the temperature is **-20°C**. The next day, it warms up by **15°C**. What is the new temperature?

☐ °C

ROMAN NUMERALS

Before Piella Bakewell's downfall, she took great pleasure is showing off her mansion's collection of ancient antiques to Wallace. Once, she even challenged Wallace to decode the mysterious Roman numerals on an old vase. Wallace was stumped by the numerals DCLXVI. Work out what this and others mean.

When reading Roman numerals, add values if smaller letters come after larger ones (like VI = 5 + 1 = 6). Subtract if smaller letters come before larger ones (like IV = 5 - 1 = 4).

I = 1, V = 5, X = 10, L = 50, C = 100, D = 500 and M = 1000.

1

Draw lines from the Roman numeral to the number.

CXCIV	CCCXLV	DCXVI	DCCLIX	CDLXXXII	CMXCIX
345	482	759	999	194	616

2

Complete the table. One has been done for you.

	194	=	CXCIV	=	One hundred ninety-four
a.		=	CCCXLVIII	=	
b.	792	=		=	
c.		=		=	Nine hundred forty-four
d.	476	=		=	
e.		=		=	Eight hundred thirty-one

3

Put these numbers in order from smallest to largest.

a.	CDL	M	XCIX	CCC				
b.	DCC	IV	CM	LX				
c.	DCXIV	IX	CCCLX	D				
d.	LXXX	M	CXLIV	DCXL				
e.	CDXXII	DCCC	XIX	CMXC				

ADDITION

SCAN CODE

On the Moon, Wallace is wondering how many cheese spikes he can fit into the rocket to bring back to Earth. Can you help him work out the total number of cheese spikes?

When using the column addition method, you start with the ones column and work to the left to the tens, hundreds then thousands column. When you add more than nine in one column, you 'carry' over the first digit to the column on its left.

	Th	H	T	O
	3	5	6	7
+	4	6	4	4
	8	2	1	1
		1	1	1

1

Work out the total numbers of cheese spikes.

a.
```
    4 3 8 6
  + 2 5 1 7
  _________
  _________
```

b.
```
    4 7 3 8
  + 3 2 4 9
  _________
  _________
```

c.
```
    5 6 2 7
  + 1 8 7 4
  _________
  _________
```

d.
```
    4 2 1 8
  + 3 9 6 5
  _________
  _________
```

2

As he worked out the totals, Wallace got tea stains over some of the numbers. Use your knowledge of addition to work out the missing numbers.

a.
```
    6 8 4 5
  + 2 □ 7 □
  _________
    □ 2 2 1
  _________
```

b.
```
    7 2 □ □
  + □ 8 4 7
  _________
    9 1 4 0
  _________
```

c.
```
    5 6 □ 4
  + 2 4 9 8
  _________
    8 □ 3 □
  _________
```

d.
```
    □ 4 2 1
  + 1 3 □ 2
  _________
    9 □ 7 3
  _________
```

3

Look at the number pyramid below and fill in the missing answers. Add the numbers and put the answer in the box above. The first one has been done for you.

5,842				
2,314	3,528	4,197	2,489	3,162

SUBTRACTION

Wallace built a cheese-sorting contraption to divide his cheese wedges into two stacks. Unfortunately, it miscalculated and the stacks are not equal. Help Wallace work out how many wedges there are in each pile.

When you carry out subtraction you always start with the ones column and work to the left. If you do not have enough to subtract from in the ones column, you can 'borrow' from the tens column. If you do not have enough in the tens column, you can 'borrow' from the hundreds column, and so on.

	Th	H	T	O
	9	3 ~~4~~	15 ~~6~~	12
-	3	1	8	6
	6	2	7	6

1

Wallace knows the number of cheese wedges he started with and has counted the number in one pile. Work out how many wedges are in the other pile.

a.
```
  7 8 2 5
- 4 6 3 9
_________
```

b.
```
  6 9 0 4
- 2 7 5 8
_________
```

c.
```
  8 3 1 6
- 3 4 2 7
_________
```

d.
```
  9 7 4 2
- 5 8 5 6
_________
```

2

Wallace has been busy working out the calculations but asks Gromit to check them to see if he is correct. Put a tick below each of the subtractions Wallace has got correct.

a.
```
  8 7 4 2
- 5 6 8 4
_________
  3 1 4 2
```
☐

b.
```
  7 9 3 5
- 3 4 6 7
_________
  4 4 6 8
```
☐

c.
```
  9 2 0 6
- 4 7 3 8
_________
  5 5 3 2
```
☐

d.
```
  6 8 5 1
- 2 9 7 3
_________
  3 8 7 8
```
☐

3

Answer the questions about Wallace, Gromit and the cheese.

a. Wallace's pile of cheese has **7,834** pieces but he only needs **4,678**. How many pieces are unused? ☐

b. Gromit bakes **9,206** cheese scones but the order was only for **2,749**. How many are left? ☐

c. Wallace orders **8,592** cheese blocks for an experiment but only **3,758** arrive due to a delay. How many remain to be delivered? ☐

d. A cheese fair has **6,731** visitors in the morning and **4,582** in the afternoon. How many more visitors came in the morning? ☐

MENTAL ADDITION

Wendolene is knitting a giant blanket and needs to calculate how many balls of wool she'll use. With piles of wool around her, she uses her addition skills to tackle the larger numbers.

1

Help Wendolene use the simple sum to work out the related sum.

a.

14	
8	6

800	

b.

19	
11	8

	800

c.

13	
4	9

13,000	

d.

18	
10	8

180,000	

Wendolene knows that 9 + 3 = 12. She uses this knowledge to work out that 900 + 300 = 1200.

12	
9	3

SO

1200	
900	300

2

Use your mental addition strategies to work out these addition sums.

a.	45 + 35 =	450 + 350 =	450 + 356 =
b.	38 + 27 =	380 + 270 =	388 + 270 =
c.	29 + 34 =	290 + 340 =	301 + 340 =
d.	47 + 31 =	4,700 + 3,100 =	4,700 + 3,900 =
e.	23 + 67 =	230,000 + 670,000 =	230,000 + 700,000 =

3

Mentally work out the answer to these problems.

a. Wendolene starts a new project and orders **156** balls of red wool and **189** balls of blue wool. How many balls of wool does she have in total?

b. She notices **243** balls of wool in her basket and adds another **176** from her cupboard. How many are there now?

c. Wendolene's neighbour lends her **389** balls of wool, and she adds them to her **212** leftover balls. What is the total?

d. For her latest knitting project, Wendolene needs **317** balls of one type and **284** of another. How many balls will she need in total?

e. A knitting club donates **145** balls of wool, which she combines with a stash of **236** she already has. How many does she have now?

MENTAL SUBTRACTION

Feathers McGraw, the criminal mastermind, is up to his usual tricks! He's stolen several sacks of golden coins, but his escape plan hits a snag - each sack is too big to fit through the narrow drainpipe. He'll need to remove some coins from each one to make it through.

Can you figure out how many coins he will have left?

1

Use your mental maths skills to work out the number of coins Feathers has left.

	Number of coins in the sack	Number of coins removed	Number of coins left
a.	764	528	
b.	892	457	
c.	675	389	
d.	947	614	
e.	803	476	

2

Complete these number pyramids using mental subtraction.

a.

652	
237	

b.

567	
	241

c.

799	
482	

d.

401	
143	

e.

663	
389	

f.

843	
461	

3

Answer the questions about Feathers McGraw and his coins.

a. Feathers McGraw's sack originally held **784** coins. To fit through the drainpipe, he removed **329** coins. How many coins does he have left?

b. The sack contains **652** coins, but the narrow pipe means he has to leave **178** behind. How many coins does he take with him?

c. Feathers McGraw filled his sack with **915** coins, but it's too heavy! He removes **436** coins to lighten it. How many coins remain?

d. With **704** coins in his sack, Feathers realises the sack won't squeeze through unless he removes **245** coins. How many coins can he keep?

e. Feathers McGraw stashed **568** coins in his sack, but he must discard **132** to escape. How many coins does he escape with?

PROBLEM SOLVING

Use mental calculations or a written method to answer these addition and subtraction questions about the characters from Wallace & Gromit.

a. Wallace builds a machine using **2,345** bolts and **1,876** screws. Gromit notices he needs an additional **738** bolts. How many bolts and screws are there in total after Wallace adds the extra ones?

b. Preston has **4,562** cans of dog food but his lorry drops **2,319** on the way. The door wasn't fastened properly and he loses another **738**. How many are left?

c. Wendolene is knitting a scarf. She starts with **127** metres of wool, uses **84** metres, and then realises she needs another **45** metres to finish the scarf. How many metres of wool does she use altogether?

d. Piella Bakewell bakes **1,924** pies. She gives **1,678** of them away to the local fair. She later bakes another **345**. How many pies does she have now?

e. Fluffles loves a long walk each day. She likes to walk for **234** minutes around the park. If she has walked for **96** minutes how long does she have left to walk?

PRIME AND SQUARE NUMBERS

Wallace is tasting his favourite cheeses.

He gives each cheese a score out of 100 according to how tasty they are. He realises some of the cheese scores are prime numbers.

A prime number is a number that can only be divided by itself and 1 without remainders.

A square number is the result of when a number has been multiplied by itself.

1

Put a circle around all the cheese types that are prime number tasty.

4	31	5	12	37	17
11	9	15	13	21	29

2

Look at the diagram and place the numbers correctly.

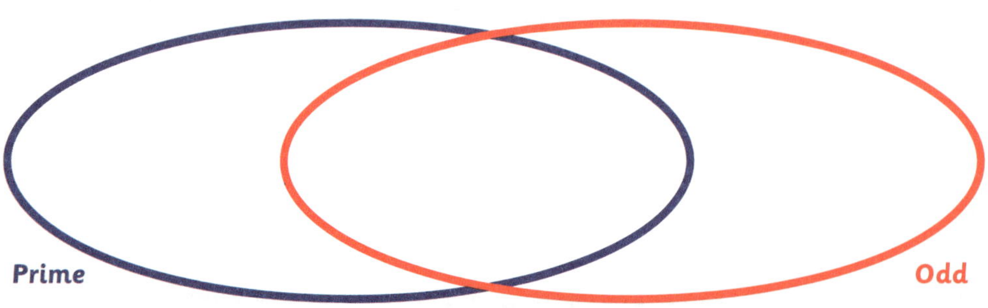

2	5	9
13	15	21
23	31	35

3

Look at the numbers and sort them into the correct column.

a.	31	32	33	34	35	36	37	38	39	40
b.	41	42	43	44	45	46	47	48	49	50
c.	51	52	53	54	55	56	57	58	59	60
d.	61	62	63	64	65	66	67	68	69	70
e.	71	72	73	74	75	76	77	78	79	80

Prime Number	Square Number

MULTIPLYING BY A ONE DIGIT NUMBER

Wallace has invented a cheese dispenser. To work out how much money he can make, Wallace knows he must count the number of cheese portions and multiply by the cost per portion. He grabs a pencil and eagerly begins to calculate.

First, multiply the ones, then the tens, and finally the hundreds.
If any answer is over 9, carry the extra digit to the next column.
Add everything together for the final answer.

In this example, Wallace has 167 cheese portions that cost £4 each.

	H	T	O
	1	6	7
x			4
£	6	6	8
	2	2	

1

Look at the cheese dispenser multiplications below and help Wallace work out how much money he will make.

a. 137 × 3 = £ ____

b. 214 × 4 = £ ____

c. 326 × 7 = £ ____

d. 451 × 8 = £ ____

2

Wallace has spilt some tea on his calculations and they have hidden some of the numbers. Can you find the missing numbers?

a. 1 3 __ × 4 = £ __ 2 8 (carry: 1)

b. 2 __ 6 × 3 = £ __ 3 8 (carry: 1, 1)

c. __ 2 7 × 6 = £ 3 1 __ 2 (carry: 1, 4)

d. __ 8 4 × 9 = £ 6 1 5 __ (carry: 7, 3)

3

Wallace has made some improvements to the machine and it is now more efficient than ever. Work out the how much money the machine makes for Wallace.

a. 1234 × 3 = £ ____

b. 2145 × 4 = £ ____

c. 3206 × 2 = £ ____

d. 1412 × 5 = £ ____

e. 1567 × 6 = £ ____

f. 2438 × 3 = £ ____

MULTIPLYING BY A TWO DIGIT NUMBER

Gromit is looking at ingredients to bake a grand cake for Fluffles. Use multiplication to calculate the quantity of ingredients he needs.

When multiplying a two-digit number by another two-digit number, you might wish to use the grid method. Fill in the missing numbers in the boxes and work out the answer by adding the numbers together.

×	30	2	
20	600	40	= 640
4	120	8	= 128
			768

1

Use the grid method for these questions.

a.

×	10	2	
30			=
4			=

b.

×	20	3	
40			=
1			=

c.

×	20	1	
30			=
2			=

Another way to work out multiplication questions is to use the column method. Remember to put a 0 down when you multiply the tens.

		2	3
	×	2	1
23 × 1 =		2	3
23 × 20 =	4	6	0
	4	8	3

2

Use the column method for these questions.

a. 44 × 22

b. 34 × 21

c. 41 × 21

d. 33 × 23

Sometimes when carrying out the column multiplication method, if the answer is greater than 9, then you have to carry a number.

			5	2
	×		3	5
52 × 5 =		2	6	0
52 × 30 =	1	5	6	0
	1	8	2	0

(carried: 1, 1)

3

Work out these more complicated multiplication questions.

a. 73 × 26

b. 58 × 32

c. 63 × 46

WRITTEN DIVISION BY A ONE DIGIT NUMBER

Preston is working out how many cans of dog food he can fit into each box. He has 124 cans to share evenly among 8 boxes. He grabs a notepad and neatly writes the numbers to work out the amount in each box.

When doing written division, you always begin on the left. For each column, if there are any remainders, they are 'carried over' to the next column.

124 ÷ 8 is written as:

```
    0  1  5 r4
8 | 1 ¹2 ⁴4
```

- 8 doesn't go into 1 so carry the 1 to the next column.
- 8 goes into 12 once and the 4 left over goes into the next column.
- 8 goes into 44 five times. The 4 left over is out at the end as a remainder.

1

Use the written method to work out the answers to these questions.

a. 6 | 2 4 5

b. 8 | 3 7 4

c. 9 | 5 6 3

d. 7 | 1 4 5 6

e. 5 | 2 3 1 2

f. 6 | 3 8 2 7

2

Use <, > or = to make these number sentences correct. Use the space for your working out.

a.	1,245 ÷ 5		9,876 ÷ 9
b.	3,612 ÷ 6		4,214 ÷ 7
c.	2,734 ÷ 4		1,248 ÷ 6
d.	4,567 ÷ 7		5,672 ÷ 8
e.	3,896 ÷ 8		1,482 ÷ 5

WRITTEN DIVISION BY A TWO DIGIT NUMBER

Preston has managed to find some larger boxes to pack his food in. He wants to share 1,624 cans equally into 12 packets. Help Preston work out the amount in each box.

This is one method Preston could have used to work out the number of cans per box.

- 12 goes into 16 once (12) with 4 remaining.
- The 4 is written underneath and the 2 in the next column is brought down to make 42.
- 12 into 42 goes 3 times (36) with 6 left over.
- The 6 is written underneath and the 4 in the next column is brought down to make 64.
- 12 into 64 goes 5 times with 4 remainders.

	0	1	3	5	r4
1 2	1	6	2	4	
	1	6			
		4	2		
		3	6		
			6	4	
			6	0	
				4	

1

Work out how many biscuits will be in each of these 12 packets. The 12 times table has been provided to help you. Use the space for your working out.

a.

12 ⟌ 1 2 4 8

b.

12 ⟌ 2 7 3 6

c.

12 ⟌ 3 4 5 2

d.

12 ⟌ 4 9 1 5

1	×	12	=	12
2	×	12	=	24
3	×	12	=	36
4	×	12	=	48
5	×	12	=	60
6	×	12	=	72
7	×	12	=	84
8	×	12	=	96
9	×	12	=	108
10	×	12	=	120
11	×	12	=	132
12	×	12	=	144

PROBLEM SOLVING

Practise your multiplication and division skills with these questions about characters from Wallace & Gromit.

a. Wallace buys **1,236** cheese crackers each month. How many does he buy in **12** months?

b. Gromit organises **2,142** books on **18** shelves. How many books does he place on each shelf?

c. Gromit bakes **1,024** rolls each day. How many does he bake in **12** days?

d. Preston is transporting **2,438** crates of dog food. Each truck holds **34** crates.
How many trucks does he need?

e. Feathers McGraw steals **1,572** gold coins and divides them into **9** bags.
How many gold coins are in each bag?

MIXED NUMBER AND IMPROPER FRACTIONS

Wallace decided to invent a special cheese cutter that would divide his favourite cheese into perfect snack portions. But in doing so, he managed to cut his cheese into improper fractions. Can you help?

A mixed number fraction and an improper fraction are different ways of writing the same amount.

A mixed number combines a whole number and a fraction. $2\frac{1}{3}$

An improper fraction has a numerator larger than its denominator. $\frac{7}{3}$

1

Look at the portions of cheese created by the 'Fraction Extractor'. Write the amount as a mixed number fraction and improper fraction.

a. 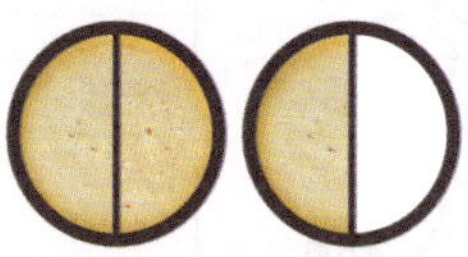

b. 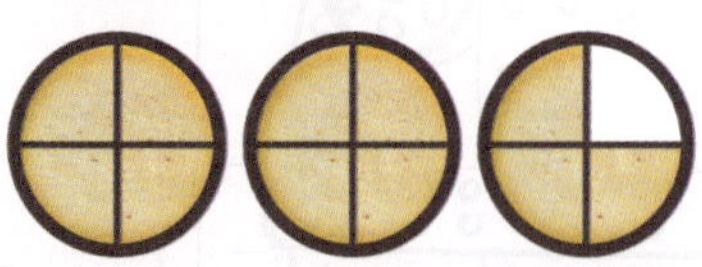

c. 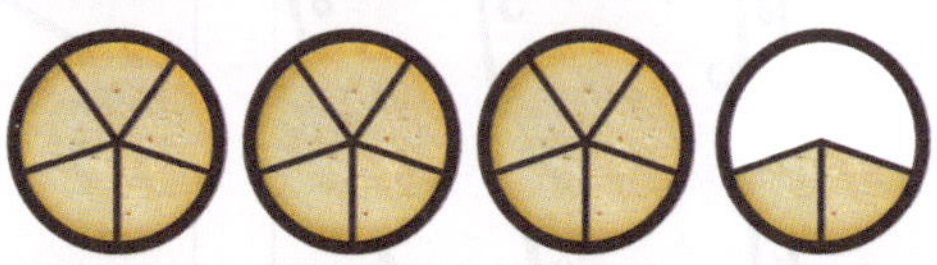

d. 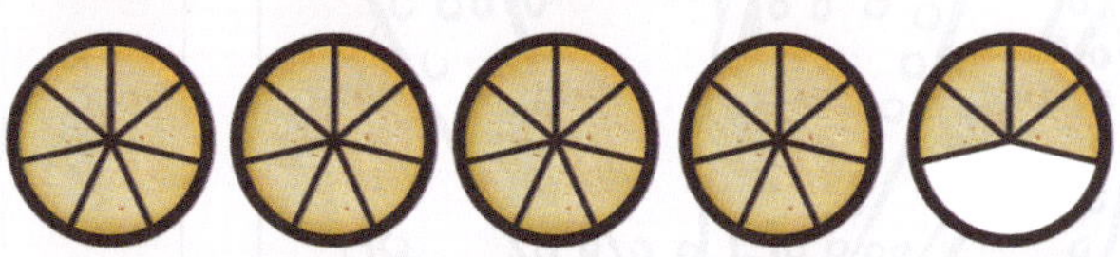

e. 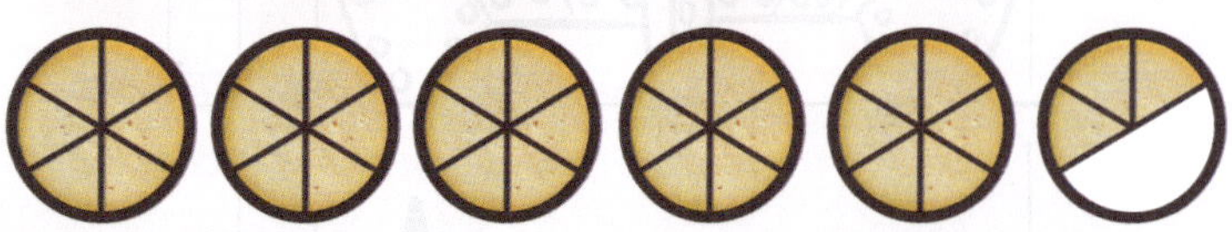

Mixed number fraction	Improper fraction

2

Convert these mixed number fractions to improper fractions.

a. $1\frac{3}{8} = \frac{\square}{\square}$ b. $2\frac{5}{6} = \frac{\square}{\square}$ c. $3\frac{4}{9} = \frac{\square}{\square}$

3

Convert these improper fractions to mixed number fractions.

a. $\frac{9}{4} = \square\frac{\square}{\square}$ b. $\frac{14}{5} = \square\frac{\square}{\square}$ c. $\frac{19}{6} = \square\frac{\square}{\square}$

ADDING AND SUBTRACTING MIXED NUMBER FRACTIONS

Piella is baking a cheese soufflé for Wallace and needs $2\frac{3}{4}$ cups of flour, but she's already added $1\frac{1}{4}$ cups. Can you help her calculate how much more she needs?

1

Work out the answers to these mixed number addition and subtraction questions. Where possible, simplify your answer.

a. $2\frac{1}{8} + 1\frac{3}{8} = \square\frac{\square}{\square} = \square\frac{\square}{\square}$

b. $5\frac{4}{10} - 2\frac{3}{10} = \square\frac{\square}{\square}$

c. $4\frac{5}{12} + 1\frac{3}{12} = \square\frac{\square}{\square} = \square\frac{\square}{\square}$

d. $6\frac{7}{14} - 3\frac{4}{14} = \square\frac{\square}{\square}$

e. $7\frac{2}{6} + 2\frac{1}{6} = \square\frac{\square}{\square} = \square\frac{\square}{\square}$

When you add or subtract mixed number fractions you need to make sure the denominator is the same.

Where possible, simplify your answer.

$$2\frac{3}{4} - 1\frac{1}{4} = 1\frac{2}{4} = 1\frac{1}{2}$$

$$2\frac{2}{10} + 3\frac{4}{10} = 5\frac{6}{10} = 5\frac{3}{5}$$

2

Work out the answer to these questions by using a common denominator. Where possible, simplify your answer.

a. $2\frac{1}{4} + 1\frac{2}{8} = \square\frac{\square}{\square} + \square\frac{\square}{\square} = \square\frac{\square}{\square} = \square\frac{\square}{\square}$

b. $4\frac{3}{5} - 2\frac{1}{10} = \square\frac{\square}{\square} - \square\frac{\square}{\square} = \square\frac{\square}{\square} = \square\frac{\square}{\square}$

c. $3\frac{1}{6} + 1\frac{2}{3} = \square\frac{\square}{\square} + \square\frac{\square}{\square} = \square\frac{\square}{\square}$

d. $5\frac{5}{12} - 2\frac{1}{6} = \square\frac{\square}{\square} - \square\frac{\square}{\square} = \square\frac{\square}{\square} = \square\frac{\square}{\square}$

e. $6\frac{3}{8} + 1\frac{5}{16} = \square\frac{\square}{\square} + \square\frac{\square}{\square} = \square\frac{\square}{\square}$

f. $3\frac{7}{9} - 1\frac{4}{18} = \square\frac{\square}{\square} - \square\frac{\square}{\square} = \square\frac{\square}{\square} = \square\frac{\square}{\square}$

3

Answer these questions about adding and subtracting mixed number fractions. Where possible, simplify your answer.

a. Piella adds $1\frac{1}{4}$ cups of sugar and $2\frac{2}{8}$ cups of cocoa powder to her mixture. How much does she add in total?

b. For the filling, Piella needs $3\frac{5}{6}$ cups of cream. She has already used $1\frac{1}{3}$ cups. How much more does she need?

c. Piella pours $4\frac{1}{5}$ cups of milk into a bowl but spills $2\frac{3}{10}$ cups. How much is left?

ADDING AND SUBTRACTING IMPROPER FRACTIONS

Piella is known for her love of cake and delicious pastries. When creating a cake, she used $\frac{11}{6}$ cups of buttercream for one layer and $\frac{4}{3}$ cups for another. How much buttercream did she use in total?

When you add or subtract improper fractions with the same denominator, then just add or subtract the numerators. If the denominators are different, you need to convert them to a common denominator.

$$\frac{4}{3} + \frac{11}{6} = \frac{8}{6} + \frac{11}{6} = \frac{19}{6}$$

1

Work out the answers to these addition or subtraction questions using improper fractions.

a. $\frac{10}{8} + \frac{17}{16} = \frac{\quad}{16} + \frac{\quad}{16} = \frac{\quad}{16}$

b. $\frac{9}{4} - \frac{9}{8} = \frac{\quad}{8} - \frac{\quad}{8} = \frac{\quad}{8}$

c. $\frac{10}{6} + \frac{13}{12} = \frac{\quad}{\quad} + \frac{\quad}{\quad} = \frac{\quad}{\quad}$

d. $\frac{20}{9} - \frac{5}{3} = \frac{\quad}{\quad} - \frac{\quad}{\quad} = \frac{\quad}{\quad}$

e. $\frac{13}{10} + \frac{7}{5} = \frac{\quad}{\quad} + \frac{\quad}{\quad} = \frac{\quad}{\quad}$

f. $\frac{5}{3} - \frac{6}{5} = \frac{\quad}{\quad} - \frac{\quad}{\quad} = \frac{\quad}{\quad}$

2

Work out the answer to each of these questions. Write the answer as an improper fraction and then change the answer to a mixed number. Where possible, simplify your answer. The first one has been done for you.

$\frac{8}{10} + \frac{7}{5} = \frac{8}{10} + \frac{14}{10} = \frac{22}{10} = 2\frac{2}{10} = 2\frac{1}{5}$

a. $\frac{6}{2} - \frac{6}{5} = \frac{\quad}{10} - \frac{\quad}{10} = \frac{\quad}{10} = \frac{\quad}{\quad} = \frac{\quad}{\quad}$

b. $\frac{5}{6} + \frac{3}{10} = \frac{\quad}{\quad} + \frac{\quad}{\quad} = \frac{\quad}{\quad} = \frac{\quad}{\quad} = \frac{\quad}{\quad}$

c. $\frac{22}{10} - \frac{3}{8} = \frac{\quad}{\quad} - \frac{\quad}{\quad} = \frac{\quad}{\quad} = \frac{\quad}{\quad} = \frac{\quad}{\quad}$

MULTIPLYING FRACTIONS

Wendolene is preparing wool for a knitting order, cutting balls into fractions of their original length. Wallace arrives with a woolly invention and needs help with measurements. Can you use multiplication of fractions to calculate the correct wool lengths?

When multiplying one fraction by another, you multiply the numerators and then multiply the denominators. Convert to a mixed number if needed. Simplify your answer.

$$\frac{2}{3} \times \frac{4}{5} = \frac{2 \times 4}{3 \times 5} = \frac{8}{15}$$

1

Draw a line from the fraction multiplication to the correct answer.

a. $\frac{1}{2} \times \frac{2}{3}$ b. $\frac{2}{5} \times \frac{3}{4}$ c. $\frac{1}{3} \times \frac{4}{5}$ d. $\frac{3}{6} \times \frac{2}{5}$

$\frac{4}{15}$ $\frac{3}{10}$ $\frac{1}{3}$ $\frac{1}{5}$

$$\frac{2}{3} \times 3 = \frac{2}{3} \times \frac{3}{1} = \frac{6}{3} = 2$$

To multiply fractions by a whole number, convert the whole number into a fraction. Then multiply the numerators and then multiply the denominators. Convert to a mixed number if needed. Simplify your answer.

2

Wendolene is dyeing wool for her shop. She uses parts of a dye bottle for each ball of wool. How much dye will she need in total? Can you help her calculate? The first one has been done for you. Remember to simplify your answers.

	Bottles of dye per ball of wool		Number of balls of wool		Bottles needed
	$\frac{2}{3}$	×	4	$\frac{2}{3} \times \frac{4}{1} = \frac{2 \times 4}{3 \times 1} = \frac{8}{3} = 2\frac{2}{3}$	$2\frac{2}{3}$
a.	$\frac{3}{5}$	×	6		
b.	$\frac{1}{2}$	×	7		
c.	$\frac{5}{6}$	×	3		
d.	$\frac{4}{5}$	×	8		
e.	$\frac{2}{3}$	×	5		

ORDERING FRACTIONS

SCAN CODE

Wendolene is sorting balls of wool by colour. Each ball is labelled with a fraction of wool remaining. She wonders which ball has the most and which has the least. Can you help her put them in order?

1

Use the fraction wall to complete these number sentences using < = and >

a. $\frac{3}{4}$ $\frac{5}{6}$

b. $\frac{7}{12}$ $\frac{2}{3}$

c. $\frac{4}{9}$ $\frac{3}{8}$

d. $\frac{5}{12}$ $\frac{3}{6}$

e. $\frac{7}{10}$ $\frac{9}{12}$

f. $\frac{8}{11}$ $\frac{10}{12}$

g. $\frac{6}{8}$ $\frac{9}{12}$

h. $\frac{5}{6}$ $\frac{7}{9}$

2

When sorting improper fractions with different denominators into order, you need to rewrite them using a common denominator. Sort the fractions below into order from smallest to largest. The first one has been done for you.

$\frac{14}{6}$ $\frac{25}{12}$ $\frac{10}{12}$ $\frac{19}{3}$ = $\frac{28}{12}$ $\frac{25}{12}$ $\frac{10}{12}$ $\frac{76}{12}$ $\frac{10}{12}$ $\frac{25}{12}$ $\frac{14}{6}$ $\frac{19}{3}$

a. $\frac{15}{8}$ $\frac{23}{4}$ $\frac{13}{2}$ $\frac{18}{4}$ =

b. $\frac{25}{16}$ $\frac{17}{8}$ $\frac{21}{4}$ $\frac{27}{8}$ =

c. $\frac{50}{20}$ $\frac{28}{5}$ $\frac{35}{10}$ $\frac{28}{10}$ =

RATIO AND PROPORTION PROBLEM SOLVING

Wallace is taking apart one of his old machines he invented a while ago. He carefully records how many of each part there is on a table.

Ratio compares one thing to another numerically. For example, in a workshop if there are 8 screws for every 5 nails, the ratio of screws to nails is 8 : 5.

1

Work out the ratio for the different parts of the machine in their simplest form. One has been done for you.

Part	Number
Cogs	8
Screws	12
Springs	4
Pulleys	3
Bolts	1
Levers	2

Cogs : Screws	2 : 3	**a.**	Springs : Pulleys	
b. Bolts : Levers		**c.**	Cogs : Springs	
d. Pulleys : Screws		**e.**	Levers : Cogs	
f. Screws : Bolts		**g.**	Cogs : Pulleys	
h. Springs : Levers		**i.**	Bolts : Screws	

2

Wallace records the quantities in ratios. Can you use the ratio information to help him figure out how many pieces of each part there are?

Part	Ratio
Springs : Cogs	3 : 1
Cogs : Levers	5 : 1
Pulleys : Levers	4 : 1
Bolts : Levers	2 : 1
Screws : Bolts	3 : 2

Part	Number
Cogs	
Screws	
Springs	15
Pulleys	
Bolts	
Levers	

3

Answer these ratio questions about other bits and pieces Gromit finds in the workshop.

a. Gromit finds **6 cogs** and **9 screws**. What is the ratio of cogs to screws in its simplest form?

b. There are **8 springs** and **4 levers** in the workshop. If Gromit finds **2 more springs**, what will the new ratio of springs to levers be in the simplest form?

c. Gromit notices that for every **3 bolts**, there are **5 pulleys** in the workshop. If there are **12 bolts**, how many pulleys are there?

PERCENTAGES

When working out discounts on prices, Wallace likes to use a calculator.

Can you work these out amounts mentally?

'Per cent' (%) means 'out of 100'. It is a whole that has been divided into 100 parts so, for example, 60% means 60 out of 100.

1

Help Wallace and Gromit work out the percentages of these amounts.

a. 10% of £30 =	b. 25% of £80 =	c. 50% of £100 =
d. 1% of £200 =	e. 10% of £150 =	f. 25% of £40 =
g. 50% of £60 =	h. 1% of £500 =	i. 10% of £70 =
j. 25% of £120 =	k. 50% of £90 =	l. 1% of £1,000 =

When working out more complex fractions of an amount, you can start by finding 10% and 1% of an amount. So to find 12% of £240

10% of £240 = £24   1% of £240 = £2.40   12% of £240 = £24 + £2.40 + £2.40 = £28.80

2

Wallace and Gromit have worked out some percentage of amounts but have mixed the answers up. Draw lines from each question to the correct answer.

a. 33% of 150	b. 12% of £200	c. 67% of £300	d. 18% of £400	e. 44% of £500	f. 29% of £600
£24	£72	£220	£49.50	£174	£201

3

Answer these percentage questions about the cheesy savings.

a. Wallace deducts **20%** from **£150** worth of mozzarella. How much is the new price?

b. If Gromit calculates **15%** off **£140** worth of Stilton, what is the discounted price?

c. If there is a **50%** discount on **£220** worth of Cheddar. How much is left to pay?

SCALE FACTORS

Gromit is looking at Wallace's plans for a handheld invention. He scales them out in his notebook. Wallace will use the plans to build the invention at full size.

The size by which Wallace must increase the measurement is called the scale factor.

If the handheld device is 2cm x 2cm and the scale factor is 2, then each measurement must be multiplied by two.

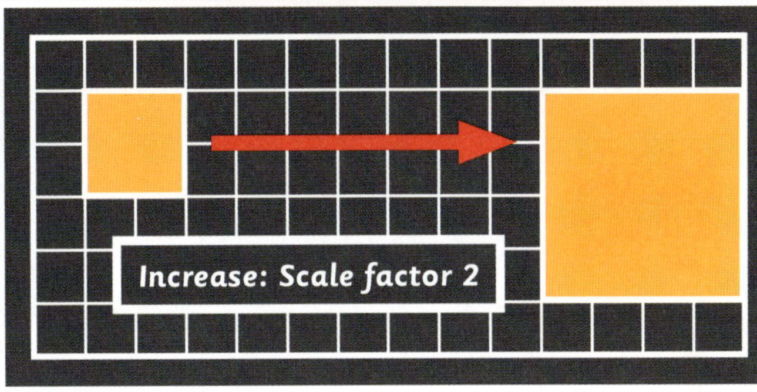

1

Wallace has drawn another design for the invention using an irregular hexagon. Work out the actual lengths by looking at the scale factors. One has been done for you.

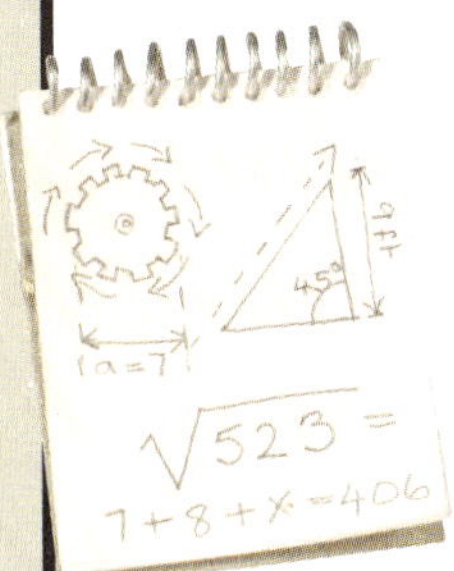

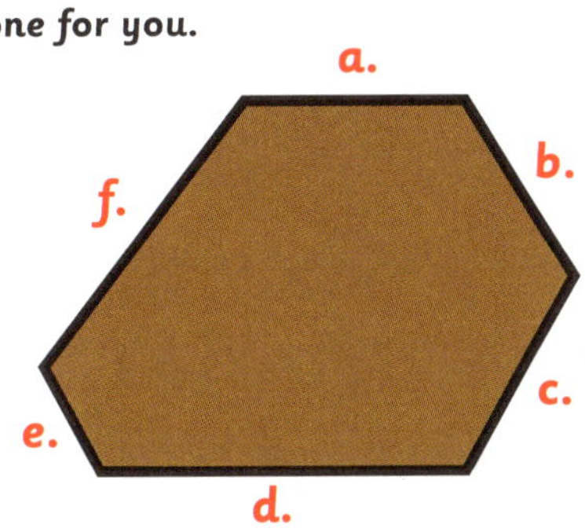

Side	Length	Scale Factor 4	Scale Factor 6	Scale Factor 10
a	5cm	20cm	30cm	50cm
b	6cm			
c	3.5cm			
d	9cm			
e	2cm			
f	7.5cm			

2

Look at the shapes. Enlarge them by redrawing them on the squared paper using a scale factor of 2.

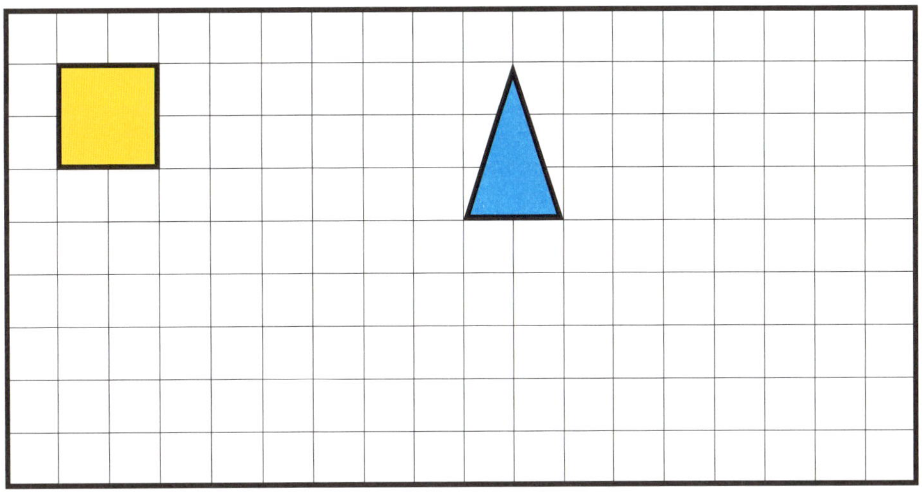

SIMPLE FORMULAE

Wallace has learned some simple algebra, and he is practising using it. Help Wallace solve these questions using simple formulas.

1

Complete the table to find the different values.

	x	3x	2x + 4	5x – 5
a.	1			
b.	4			
c.		18		
d.			24	
e.				50

2

Work out the answers to these equations. One has been done for you.

	$x = 8$	$c = 3$	$4x - 3c =$	$32 - 9 =$	23
a.	$x = 4$	$c = 5$	$3x + 2c =$		
b.	$x = 3$	$c = 2$	$5x - 6c =$		
c.	$x = 10$	$c = 12$	$2x - c + 5 =$		
d.	$x = 5$	$c = 3$	$\frac{20}{x} + 2c =$		
e.	$x = 15$	$c = 4$	$\frac{60}{x} + 5c - 10 =$		

3

Work out the value of 'c' in these equations.

a.	Work out the value of c if $a = 4$	$p = 3a + 2$	and	$c = 15 - p$	**c =**
b.	Work out the value of c if $a = 5$	$p = 4a - 1$	and	$c = 20 - p$	**c =**
c.	Work out the value of c if $a = 2$	$p = 5a + 3$	and	$c = 25 - p$	**c =**
d.	Work out the value of c if $a = 6$	$p = a + 10$	and	$c = 30 - p$	**c =**
e.	Work out the value of c if $a = 8$	$p = 2a - 4$	and	$c = 12 + p$	**c =**

NUMBER SEQUENCES

Wallace is writing some algebraic number sequences. He looks at the value of x and then works out the numbers in the sequence.

1

Complete the table to show the algebraic number sequence.

Formula

	$2x + 3$	$5x - 3x$	$3x + 5 - x$	$5x + 11$	$6x + 3x + 2$
$x = 1$	5	2		16	
$x = 2$		4			
$x = 3$					
$x = 5$					47
$x = 10$	23		25		
$x = 20$					
$x = 50$				261	
$x = 61$					
$x = 73$					
$x = 99$					893

ALGEBRA PROBLEM SOLVING

Solve these algebra word problems about the characters from Wallace & Gromit.

a. Wallace eats **3n + 5** wedges of cheese each hour.
If **n** is the number of hours, how many wedges will he eat in **4** hours?

b. Gromit calculates the number of cogs needed for an invention as **2n – 5**.
If **n = 10**, how many cogs are required?

c. Piella is baking pies. The number of pies she bakes follows the sequence:
n, **n + 3**, **n + 6**. If **n = 5**, what are the first three numbers in her sequence?

d. Preston is selling boxes of dog food for **10x – 4** pounds each.
If **x = 6**, what is the price of one box?

e. Wallace's new invention completes **5n + 1** tasks each day.
How many tasks does it complete in **7 days** if **n = 3**?

f. Wendolene knits scarves where the length of each scarf is **8k + 12** centimetres.
If **k = 4**, how long will **3 scarves** be?

g. Gromit's garden has **3n + 7** flowers planted every month.
How many flowers will there be after **5 months** if **n = 2**?

CONVERTING AND COMPARING UNITS OF MEASUREMENT

SCAN CODE

Wendolene is measuring the area of her shop window for a new display. She measures it in mm but wants to convert it to cm. Convert these measurements.

Mass
1 kilogram (kg) = 1000 g

Capacity
1 litre (l) = 1000 millilitres (ml)

Length
10 millimetres (mm) = 1 centimetre (cm)
100 cm = 1 metre (m)
1000m = 1 kilometre (km)

1

Use the signs <, > or = to complete these number sentences.

a.	300 mm		35 cm
b.	2.5 m		250 cm
c.	4 km		3500 m
d.	1.2 litres		1500 ml
e.	750 g		1 kg
f.	0.5 kg		450 g
g.	1.5 m		1200 mm
h.	6.3 litres		6000 ml
i.	0.8 km		800 m
j.	250 cm		2.6 m

2

Look at these units of measurement from the blueprints. Put them in order from smallest to largest.

a. 1.5 km, 1200 m, 120 cm, 15,000 mm

b. 1.2 kg, 0.8 kg, 0.6 kg, 400 g

c. 1.2 litres, 850 ml, 3500 ml, 3.2 litres

d. 3.5 m, 250 cm, 4500 mm, 0.45 km

e. 0.007 kg, 5 g, 0.2 kg, 2 kg

3

Answer these written questions about converting units of measurement.

a. Wendolene measures the length of a small window as **25 cm**. What is the length in millimetres?

b. One window measures **0.8 metres**. What is the length in centimetres?

c. One part of the display is **3500** millimetres long. What is the length in metres?

PERIMETER

SCAN CODE

Criminal mastermind Feathers McGraw is figuring out how to protect everything he has stolen. He starts by calculating the perimeter of his top-secret hideout to build a secure fence around it.

Perimeter is the distance around the edges of a shape.
In the example this is 5cm + 2cm + 5cm + 2cm = 14cm

1

Calculate the perimeters for these top-secret hideouts. 1 square = 1m.

a.

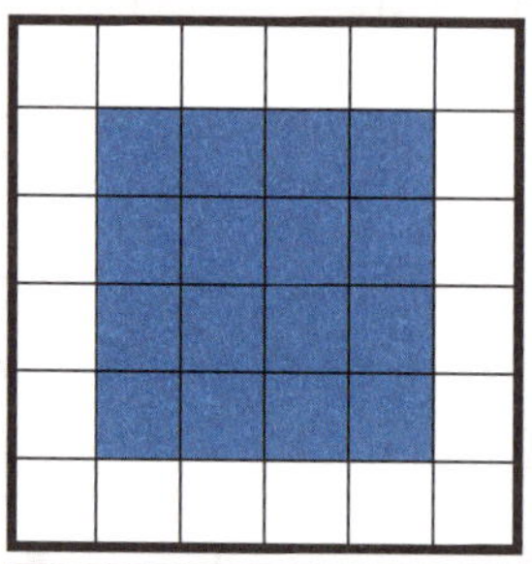

m

b.

m

c.

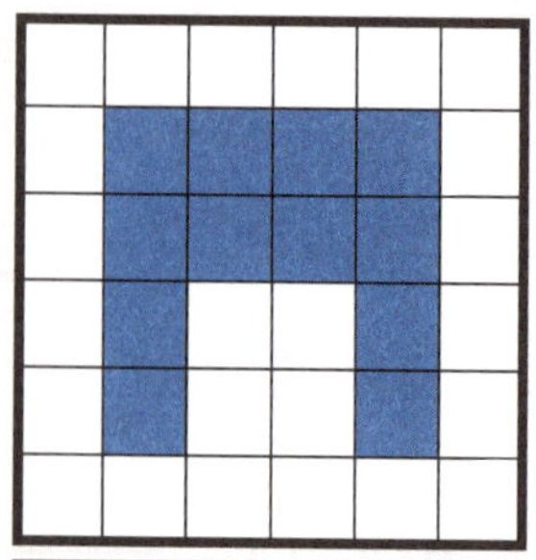

m

d.

m

e.

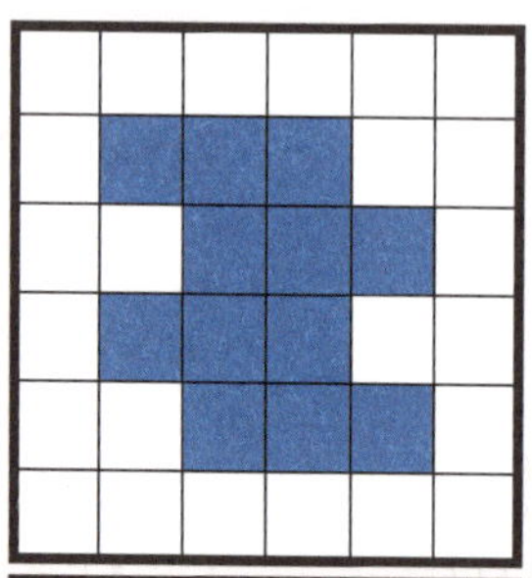

m

f.

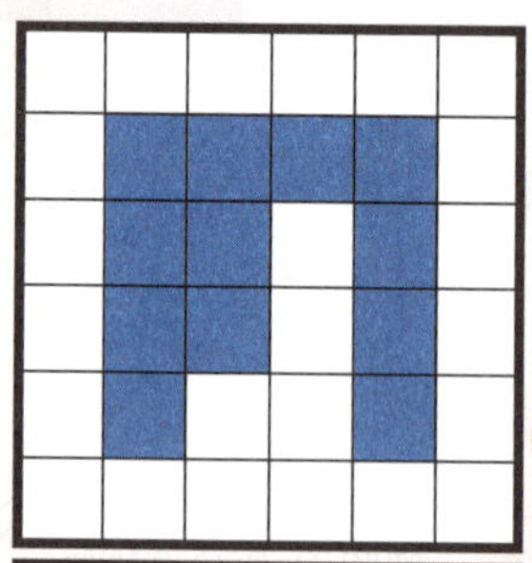

m

2

Work out the perimeter of these shapes. Look carefully at the measurements to work out the ones that are missing.

a.

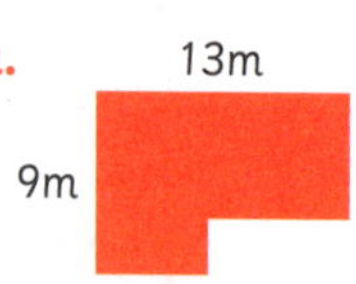

m

b.

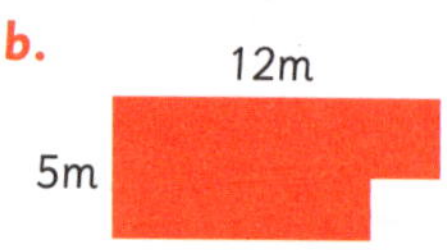

m

c.

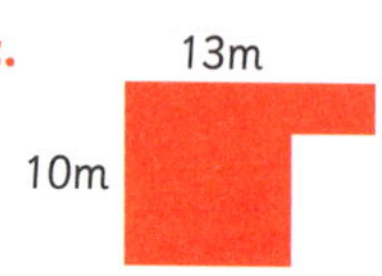

m

AREA

Feathers McGraw wants to make his secret hideout more comfortable by laying carpet. He knows that area is the amount of space something covers. Can you calculate the area of carpet needed for these rooms?

1

The carpet is shaded in blue. Calculate the area of carpet needed for each room in the top-secret hideout. 1 square = 1m².

a.

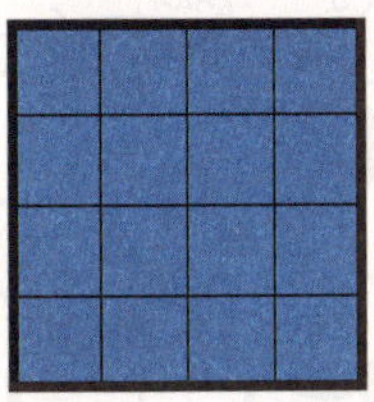

m^2

b.

m^2

c.

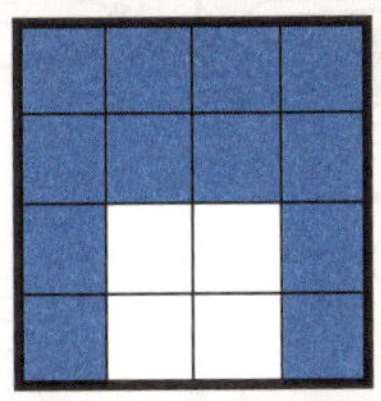

m^2

d.

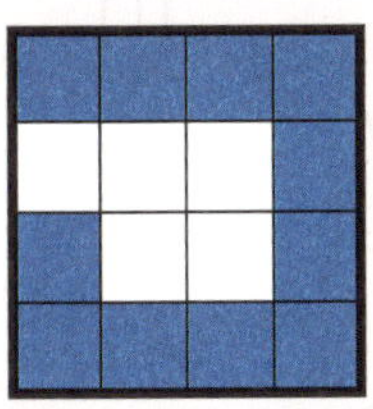

m^2

e.

m^2

f.

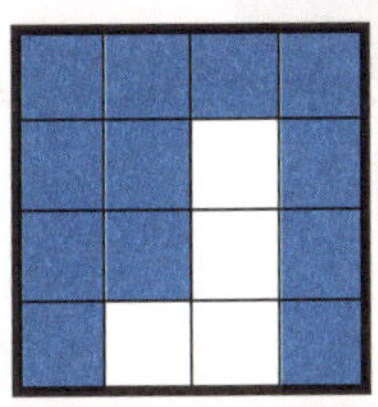

m^2

2

Feathers realises that some of his rooms are made up from triangles. Work out the area of these triangles by counting the full squares and the half squares. 1 square = 1m².

a.

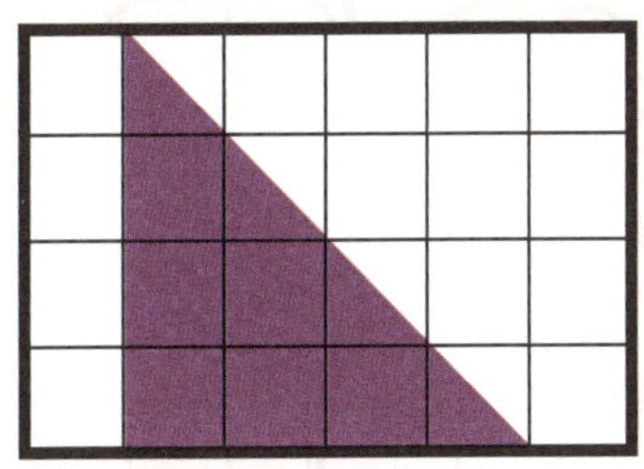

m^2

b.

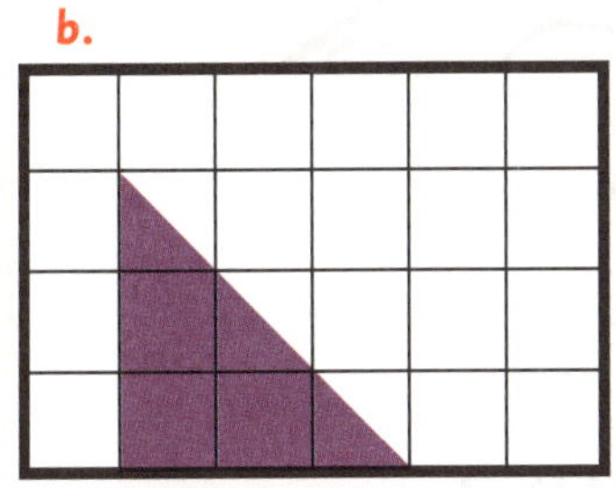

m^2

c.

m^2

3

Use the measurements to work out the area of these triangles.

a.

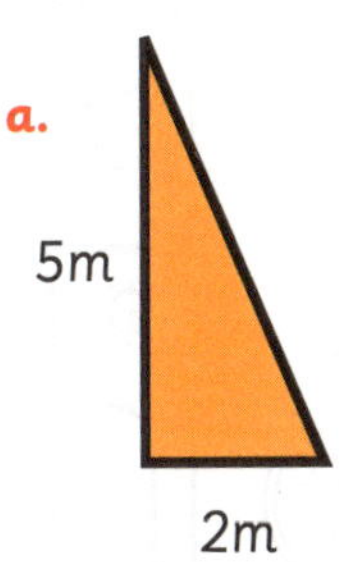

m^2

b.

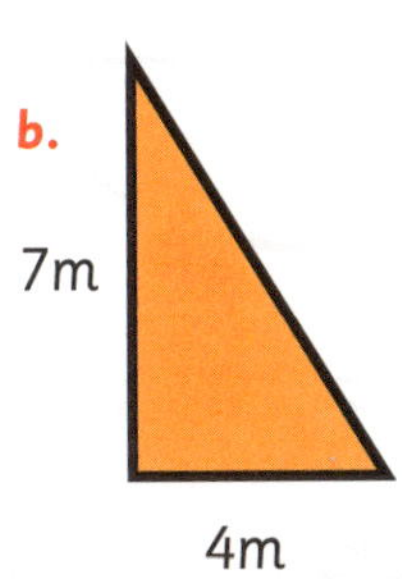

m^2

c.

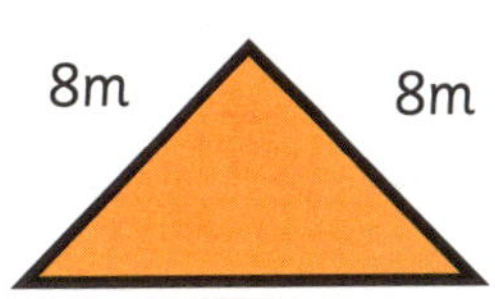

m^2

AREA

Feathers McGraw decides to make some changes and rearrange the furniture in his living quarters. Help him calculate the area of the furniture in the room so he can plan out the new design.

The side of each square is 0.2m long.

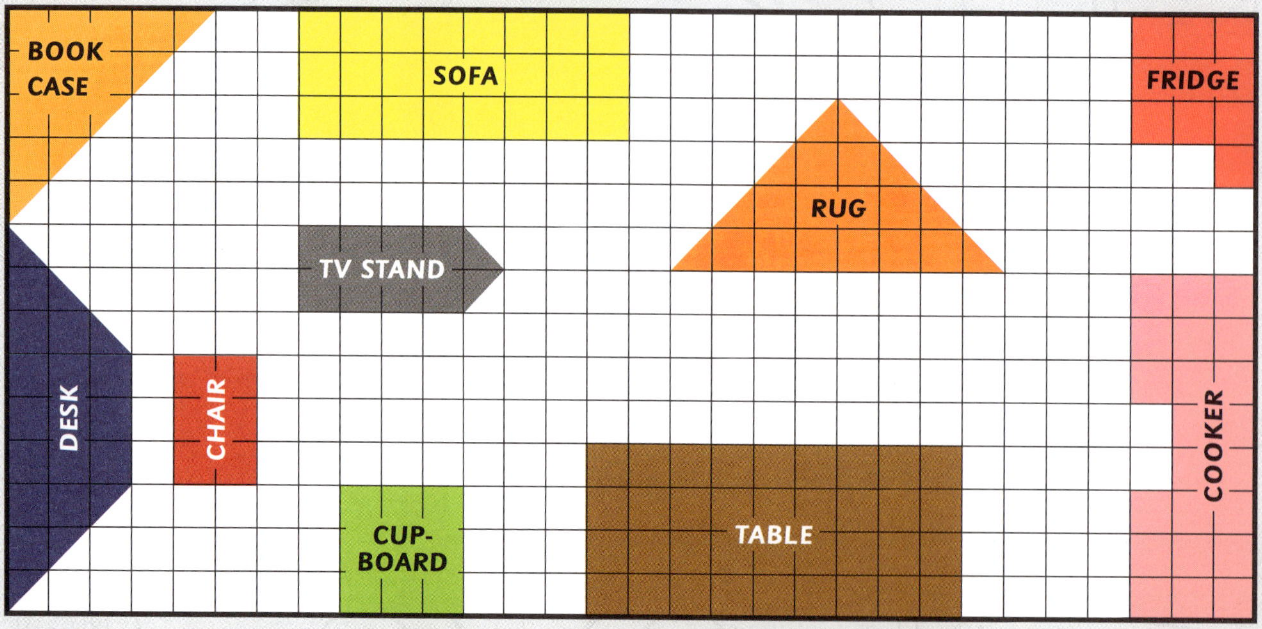

Table	m^2	Sofa	m^2	Cupboard	m^2
Chair	m^2	Bookcase	m^2	Desk	m^2
Rug	m^2	Fridge	m^2	Cooker	m^2
		Television stand	m^2		

MILES AND KILOMETRES

Wallace and Gromit are running a 'Dough to Door' delivery service from their Top Bun bakery. The sat nav they use only calculates the distance in kilometres.

Gromit knows that 1 mile = 1.6 km.

1

Look at these distances and convert them to miles or kilometres.

	miles		km		miles		km
a.	6.25	=		**f.**	2.5	=	
b.		=	2.8	**g.**	7	=	
c.	0.25	=		**h.**		=	8.8
d.	3.5	=		**i.**	8.25	=	
e.		=	7.6	**j.**		=	2.4

2

Use <, > or = to make these number sentences correct.

a.	5 km		3 miles	**f.**	12 km		7.5 miles
b.	10 km		6.2 miles	**g.**	20 km		12 miles
c.	8 km		5 miles	**h.**	3 km		1.9 miles
d.	2 km		1.5 miles	**i.**	7 km		4.5 miles
e.	15 km		9 miles	**j.**	25 km		15.5 miles

3

Answer these questions about the 'Dough to Door' delivery service.

a. The first delivery is **8 km** away. Gromit wonders how far this is in miles. Is the delivery more than **5 miles** away?

b. The next delivery is **4.8 km** away. Wallace wonders if the distance is less than **3 miles** away. Is it?

c. The final delivery is **12.8 km** away. Gromit is planning the route and converts the distance into miles. How far is it in miles?

ANGLES

Wallace is looking at plans for a new invention. He notices angles of different sizes on the plan. He sees sharp angles (acute), wide ones (obtuse), a perfect corner (right angle), and a huge curve (reflex).

Right angle

A right angle is exactly 90°. A square is made up of 4 right angles.

Acute angle

An acute angle is any angle which is smaller than 90°.

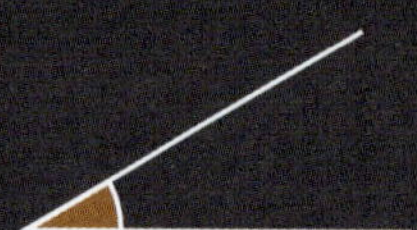

Obtuse

An obtuse angle is any angle between 90° and 180°.

Reflex angle

A reflex angle is any angle between 180° and 360°.

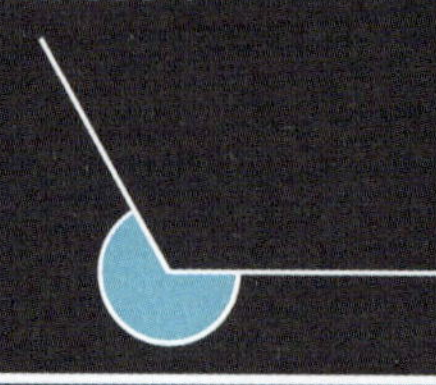

1

Look at these angles and write down what type of angle they are – acute, right, obtuse or reflex.

a.

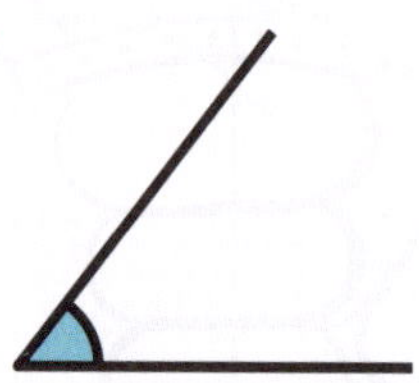

b.

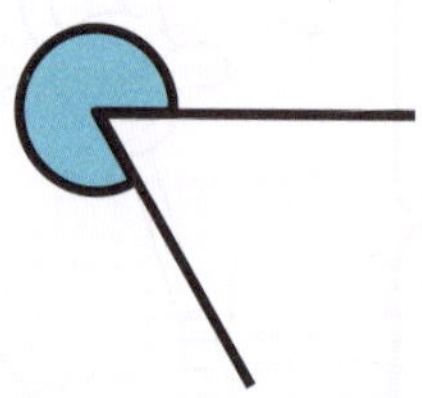

c.

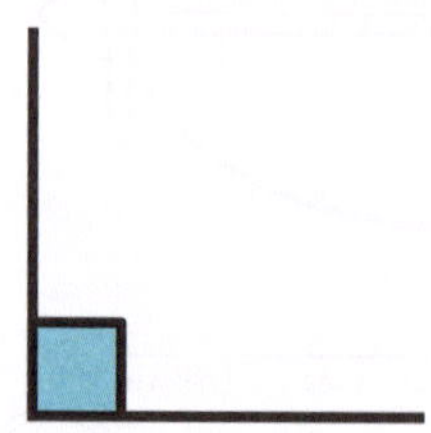

d.

e.

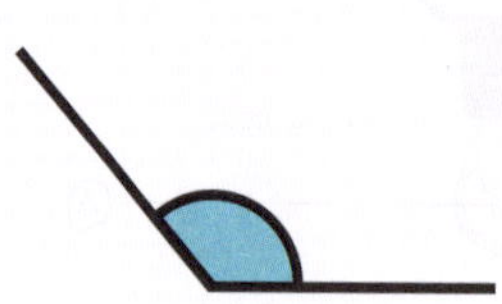

f.

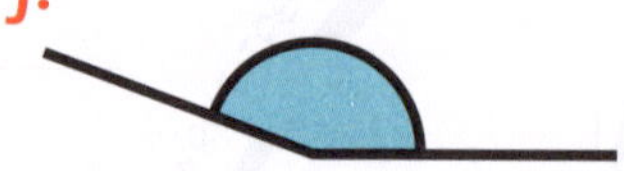

g.

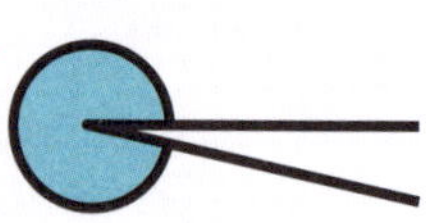

h.

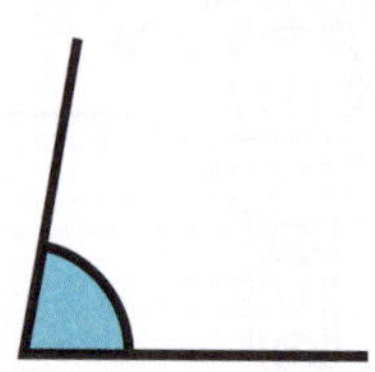

i.

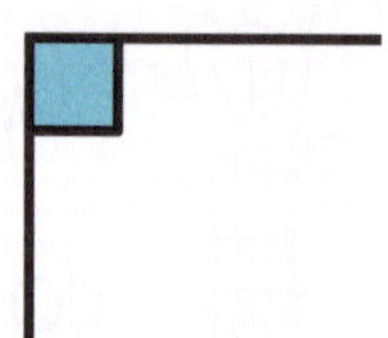

ANGLES

Wallace looks at his plan and begins to estimate the size of each of the angles in degrees.

1

Look at the angles below. Estimate the size of each angle, then draw a line from the angle to the measurement.

a. b. c. d. e.

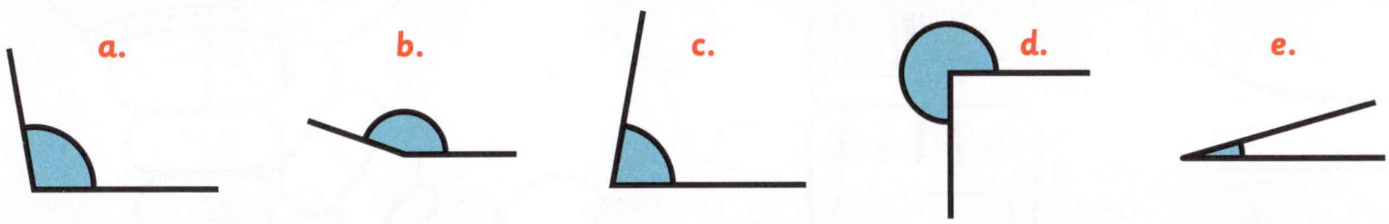

165°	15°	100°	80°	270°

2

Wallace looks at the sum of the interior angles of a regular shape. Look at the shapes and work out the value of each interior angle.

a.

Total degrees = 360°

One angle =

b.

Total degrees = 360°

One angle =

c.

Total degrees = 180°

One angle =

d.

Total degrees = 540°

One angle =

e.

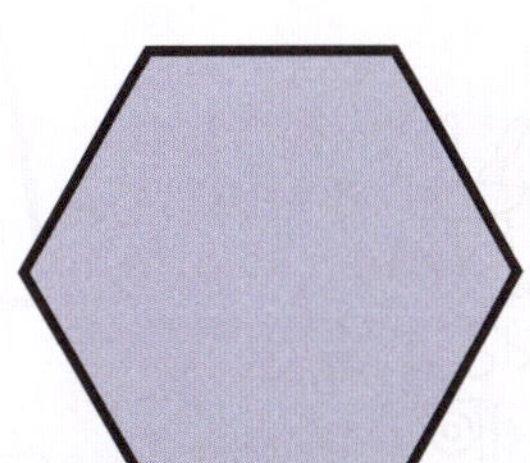

Total degrees = 720°

One angle =

f.

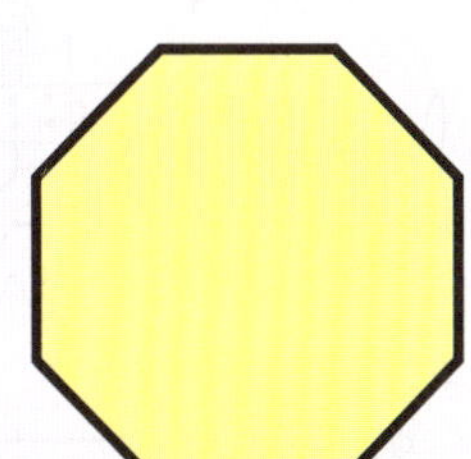

Total degrees = 1080°

One angle =

MISSING ANGLES

When looking at plans for an invention, Wallace notices some of the angles on his design are missing. Help him find the missing angles.

1

Wallace knows there are 360° in a circle. Help him work out the missing angles.

a.

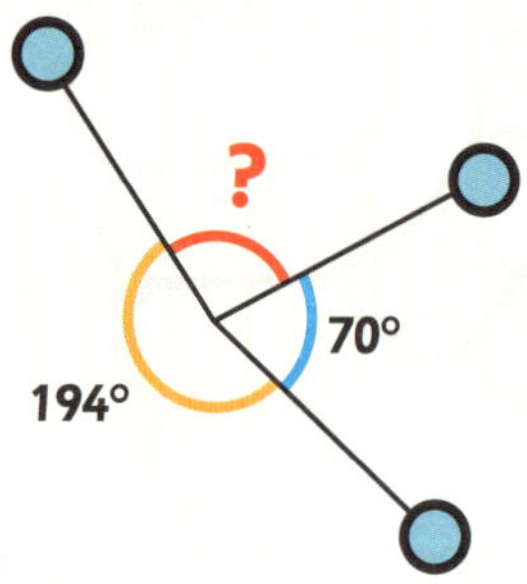

b.

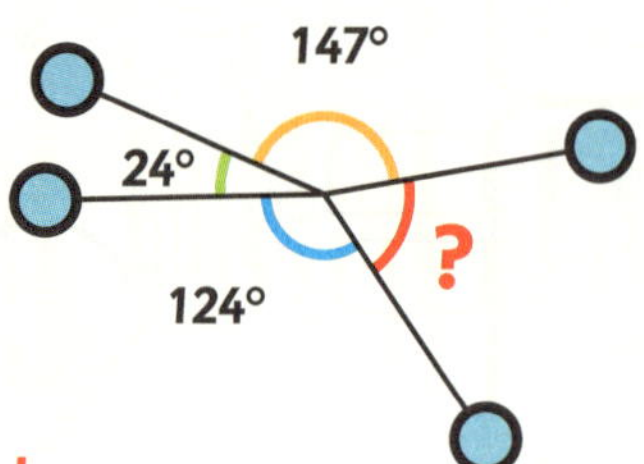

c.

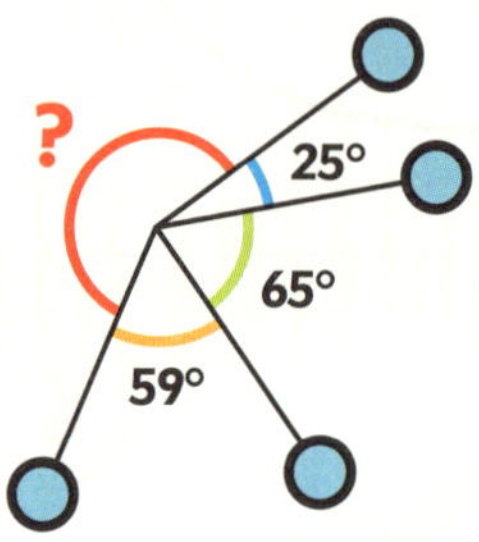

d.

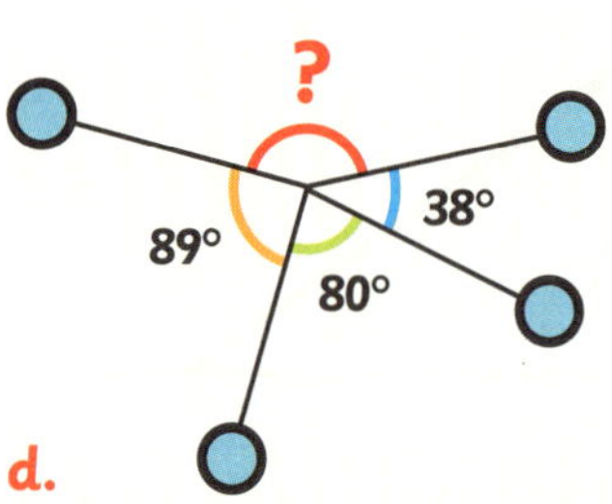

e.

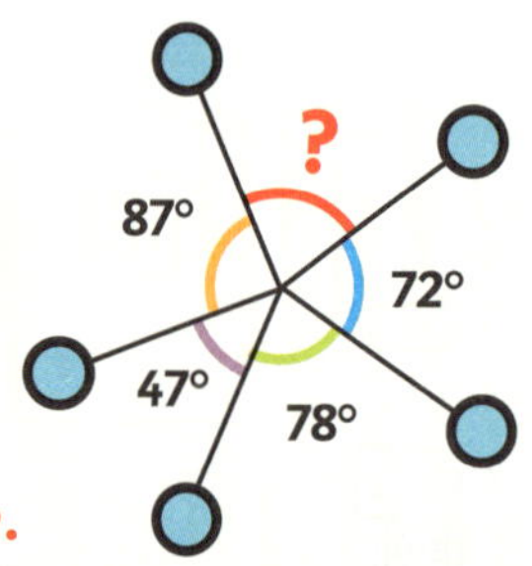

f.

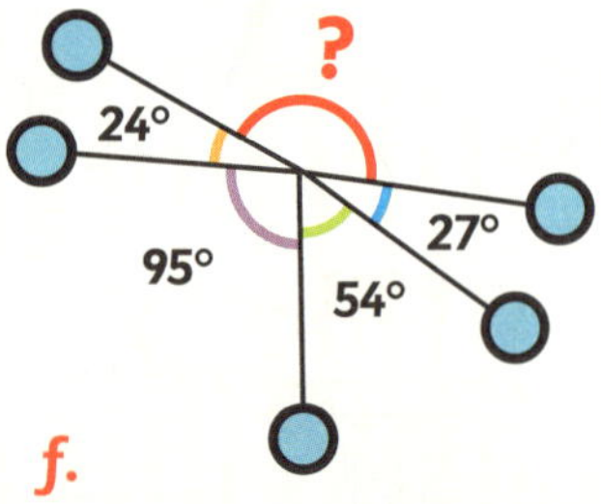

2

In these diagrams the opposite angles are the same. Write down the missing angles.

a.

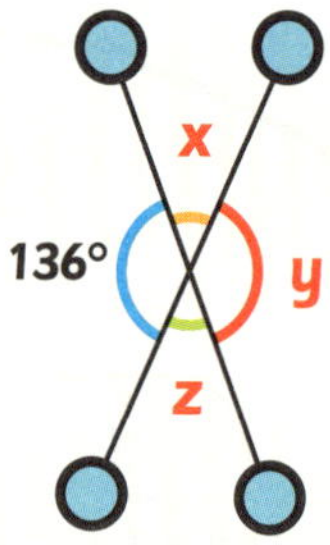

x =
y =
z =

b.

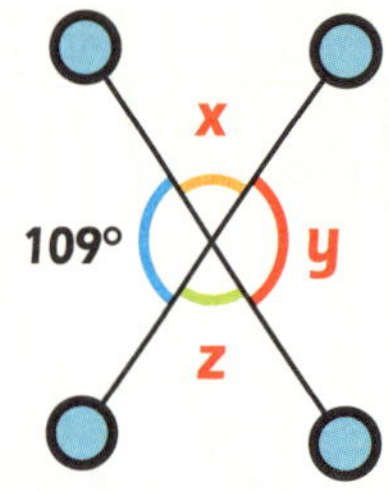

x =
y =
z =

c.

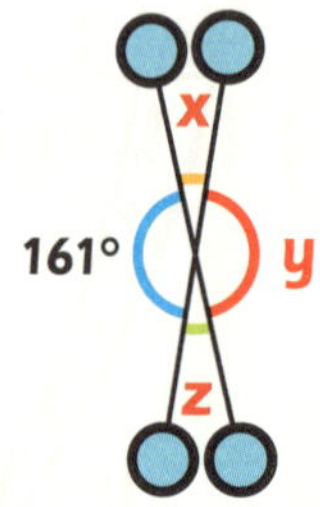

x =
y =
z =

d.

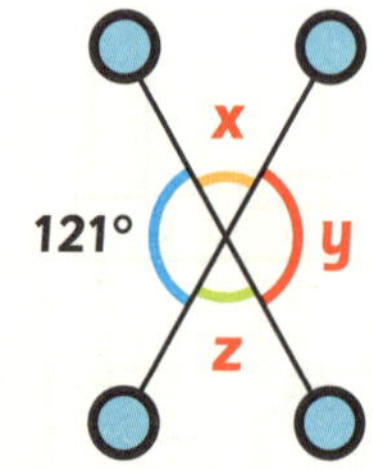

x =
y =
z =

MISSING ANGLES

Wallace realises he has used lots of triangles in his design. Look at the triangles below and work out the missing angles. Remember, interior angles of a triangle always equal 180°.

1

Work out the missing angle for each of these triangles. Write each answer underneath.

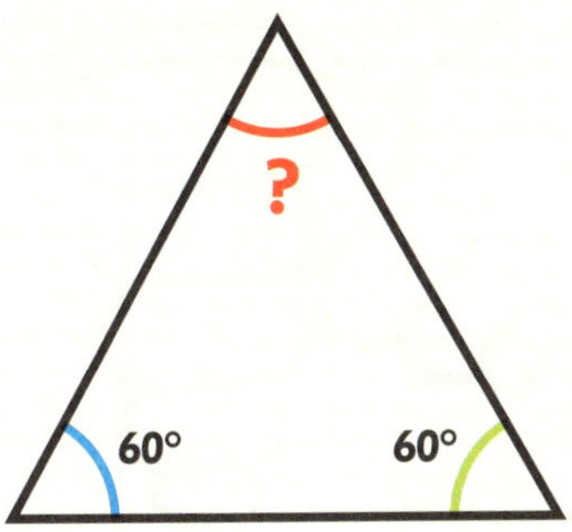

a. Angle =

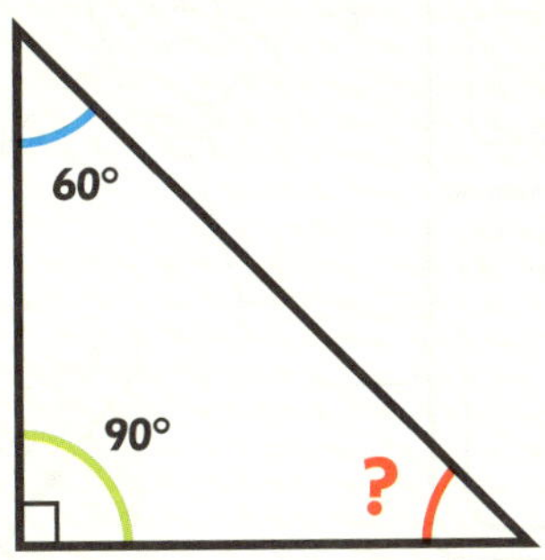

b. Angle =

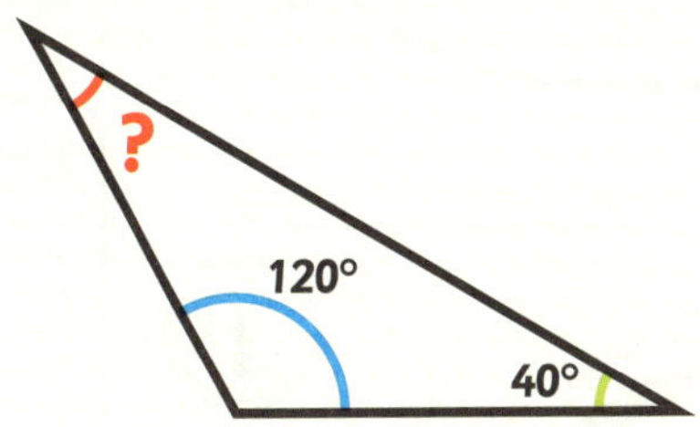

c. Angle =

2

The interior angles of a quadrilateral, both regular and irregular, always equal 360°. Put a tick below the shapes where the angles have been recorded correctly, and therefore equal 360°, and a cross where they do not.

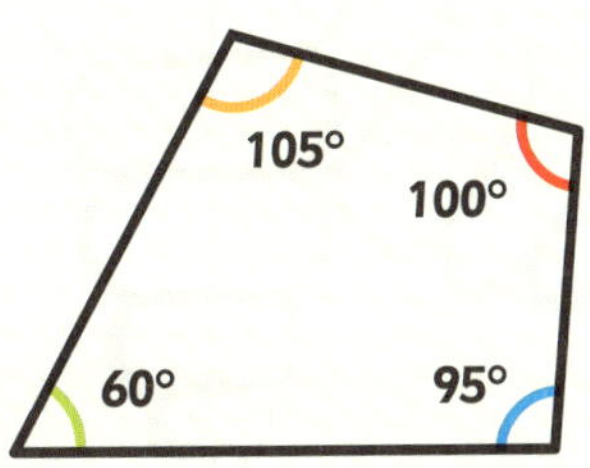

a.

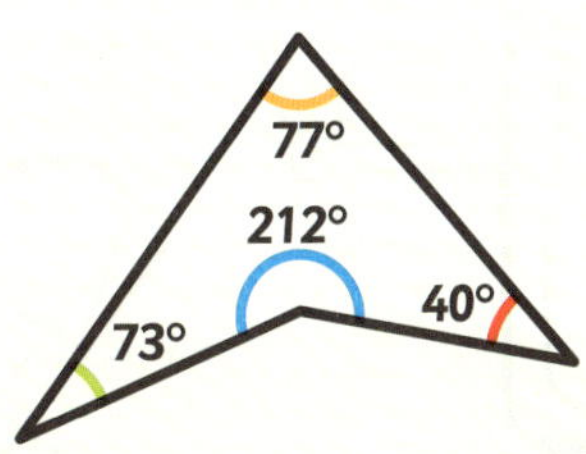

b.

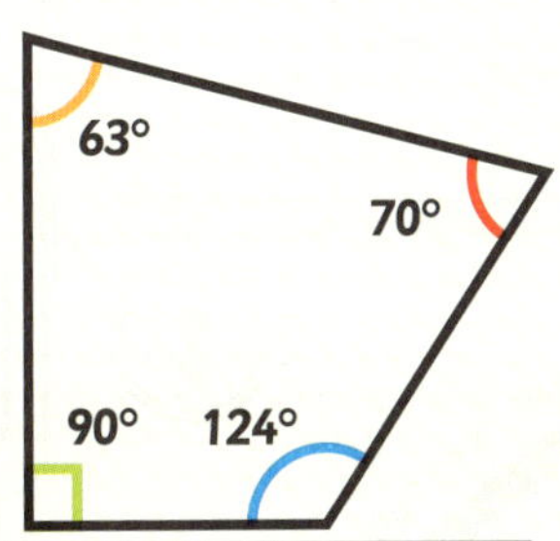

c.

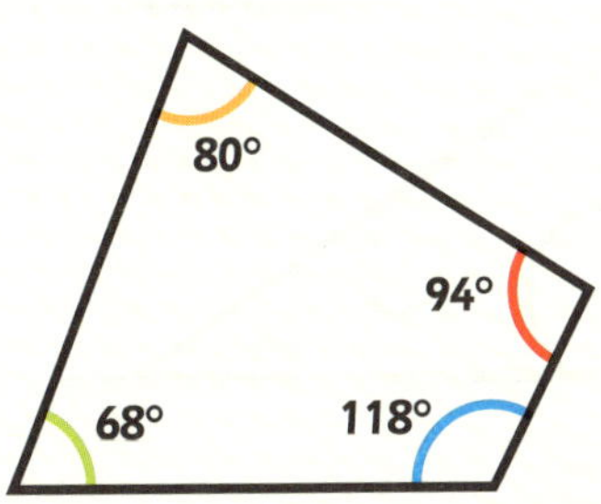

d.

e.

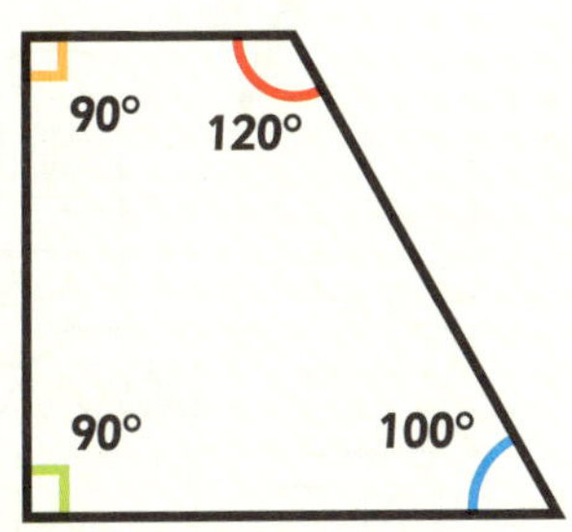

f.

REFLECTION

Gromit wants to create a symmetrical garden. Can you help him lay a path so that each side is a perfect reflection of the other?

When an object is reflected, it needs a mirror line. The object's size doesn't change, the image just appears flipped so that every point on the shape is the same distance away on the other side of the mirror line.

1

Look at the first half of each path that Gromit has designed. Shade the reflection of the other side.

a.

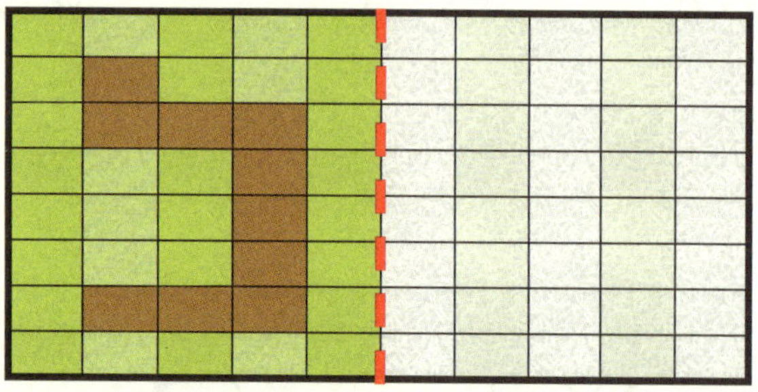

b.

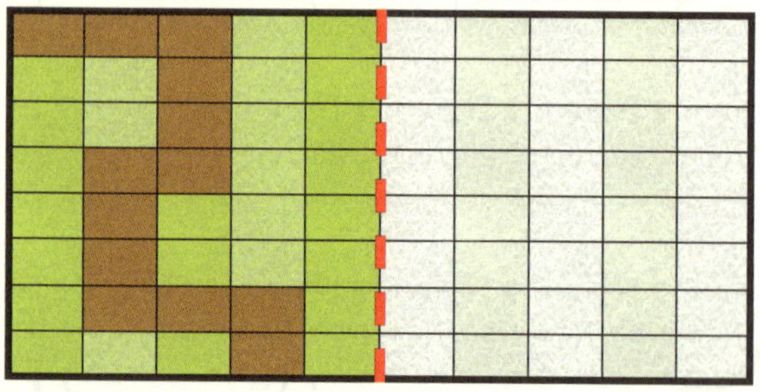

c.

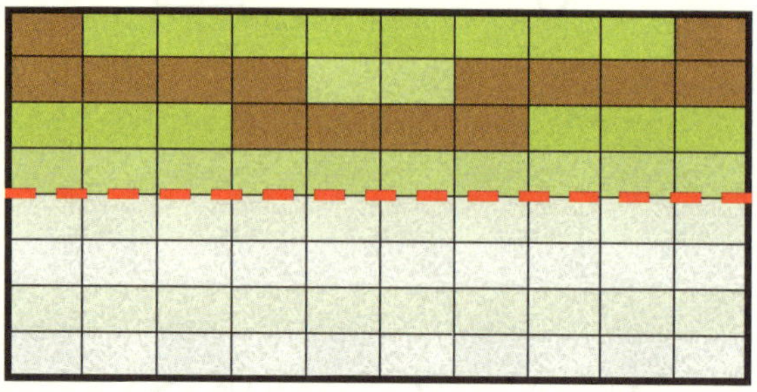

d.

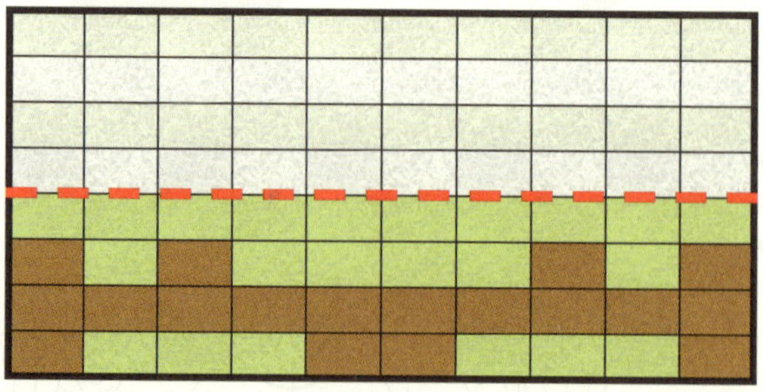

2

After finishing the paths, Gromit plants some flowers. Put a tick next to the reflected flowers.

TRANSLATION

Feathers McGraw is plotting to move some jewels across the museum without setting off the alarm. He carefully plans the translation path he needs to take to avoid detection.

A translation is a type of transformation. It moves a shape up, down or from left to right, but it does not change its appearance in any other way.

1

Feathers has planned out the translations he needs to take for each of the jewels. Look at the translations from A to B and write them down.

a.

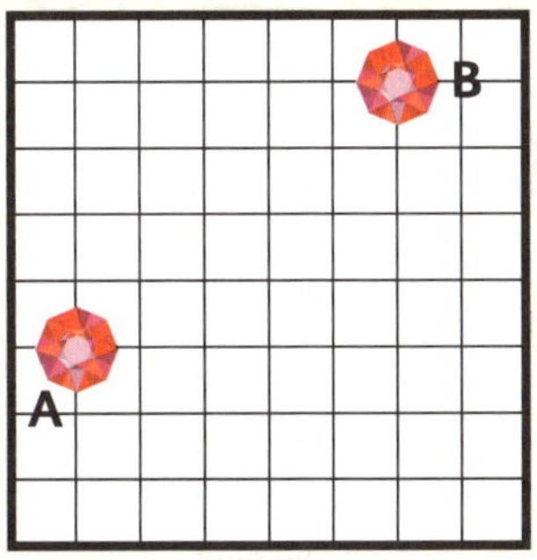

right ___ up ___

b.

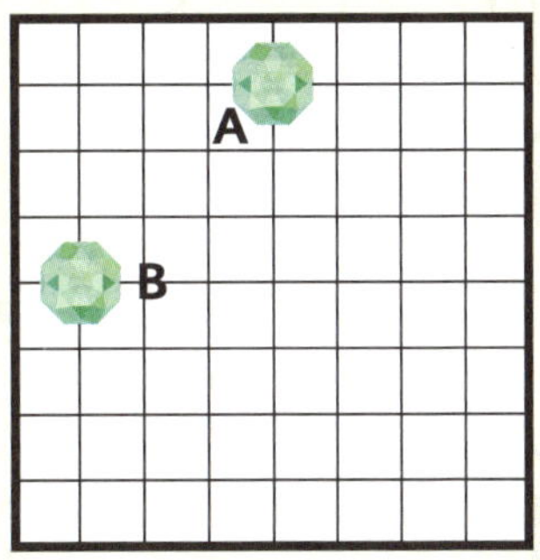

left ___ down ___

c.

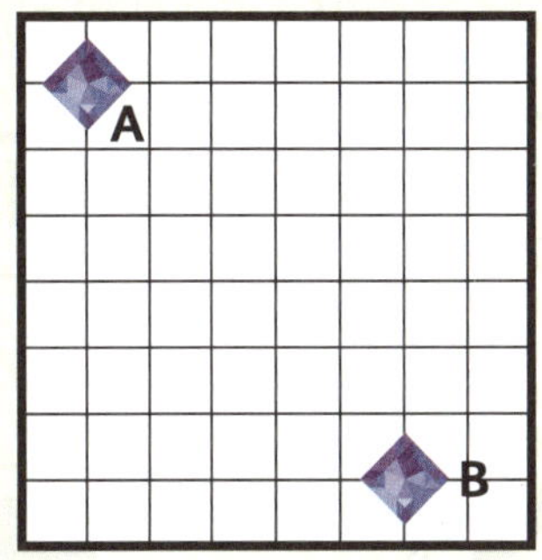

down ___ right ___

d.

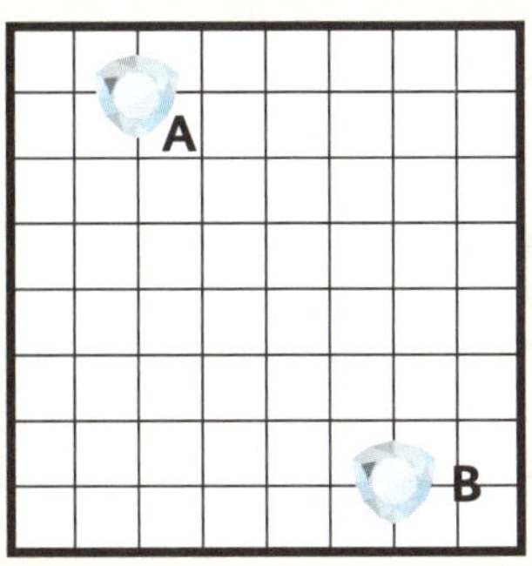

down ___ right ___

e.

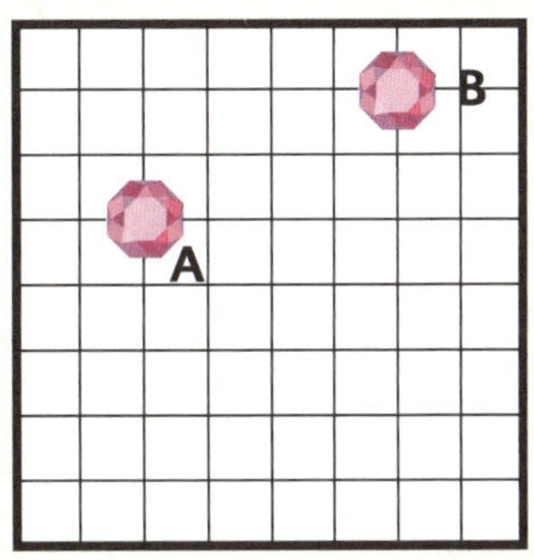

right ___ up ___

f.

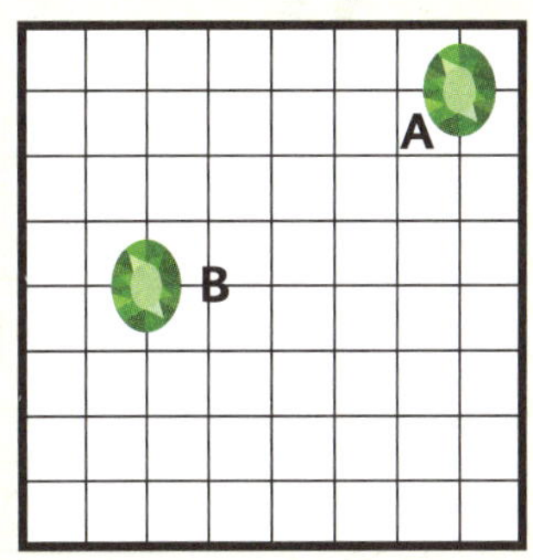

down ___ left ___

2

Look at the instructions and translate the shapes to their new positions.

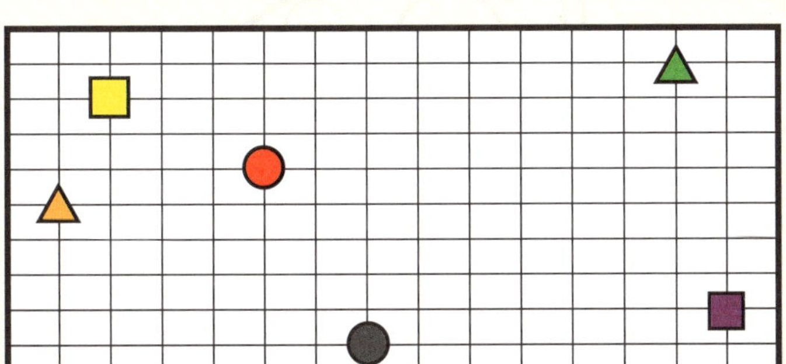

- ■ (yellow) → 8 ↓ 4
- ▲ (green) ↓ 6 ← 10
- ● (red) → 3 ↑ 3
- ■ (purple) ← 5 ↓ 1
- ▲ (orange) → 10 ↑ 3
- ● (grey) ← 2 ↑ 2

COORDINATES

Wallace is tidying up the house while Gromit is asleep. To ensure he doesn't bump into anything and wake Gromit up, Wallace carefully notes down the coordinates of various objects on a grid.

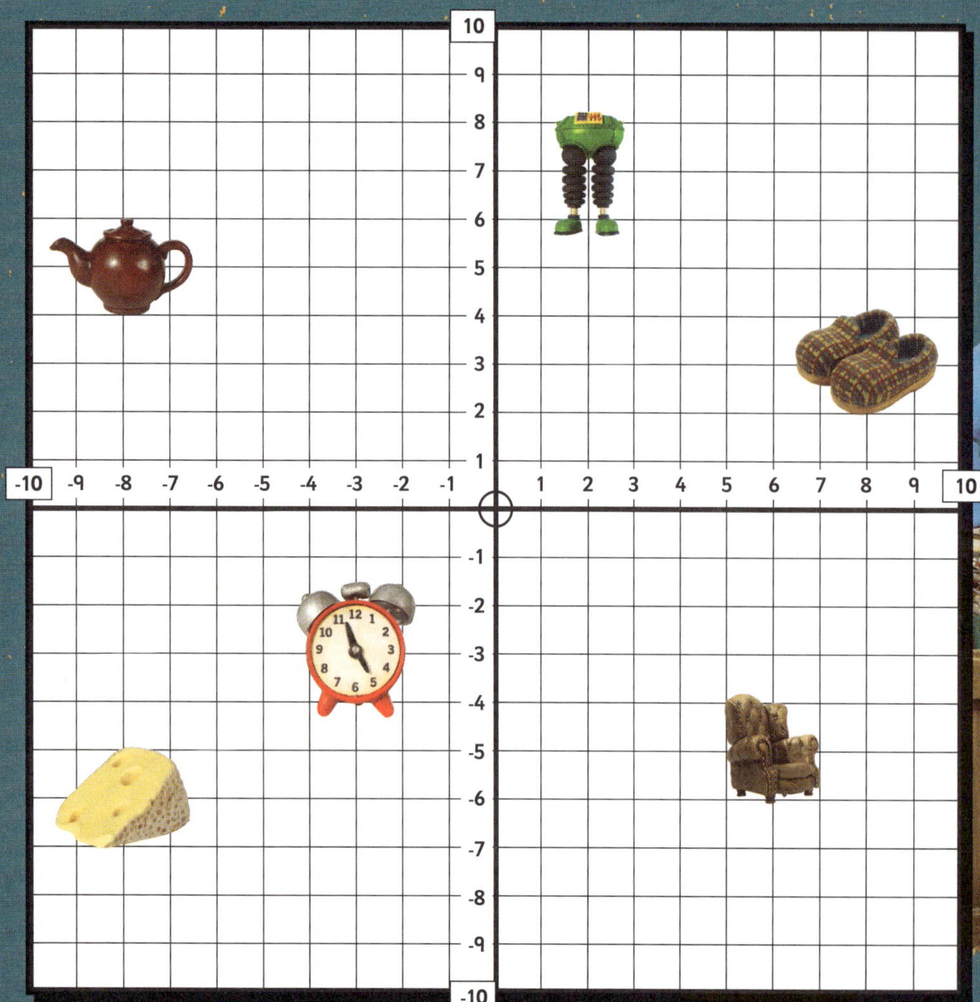

1

Look at the coordinates and circle what can be found there.

a. (-3, -3) 

d. (-8, -6) 

b. (8, 3) 

e. (2, 7) 

c. (-8, 5) 

f. (6, -5) 

COORDINATES

Wallace is a brilliant inventor, but he's far from tidy. After a busy day in the workshop, tools are scattered everywhere. Gromit surveys the chaos and decides to reorganise where Wallace hangs his tools to keep things tidier.

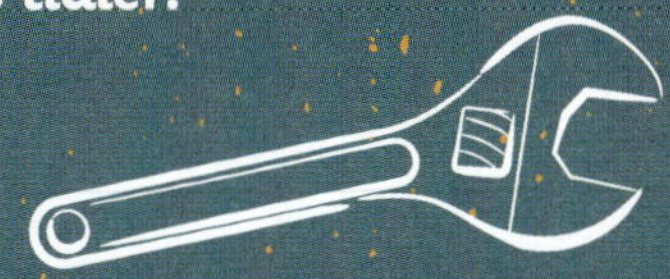

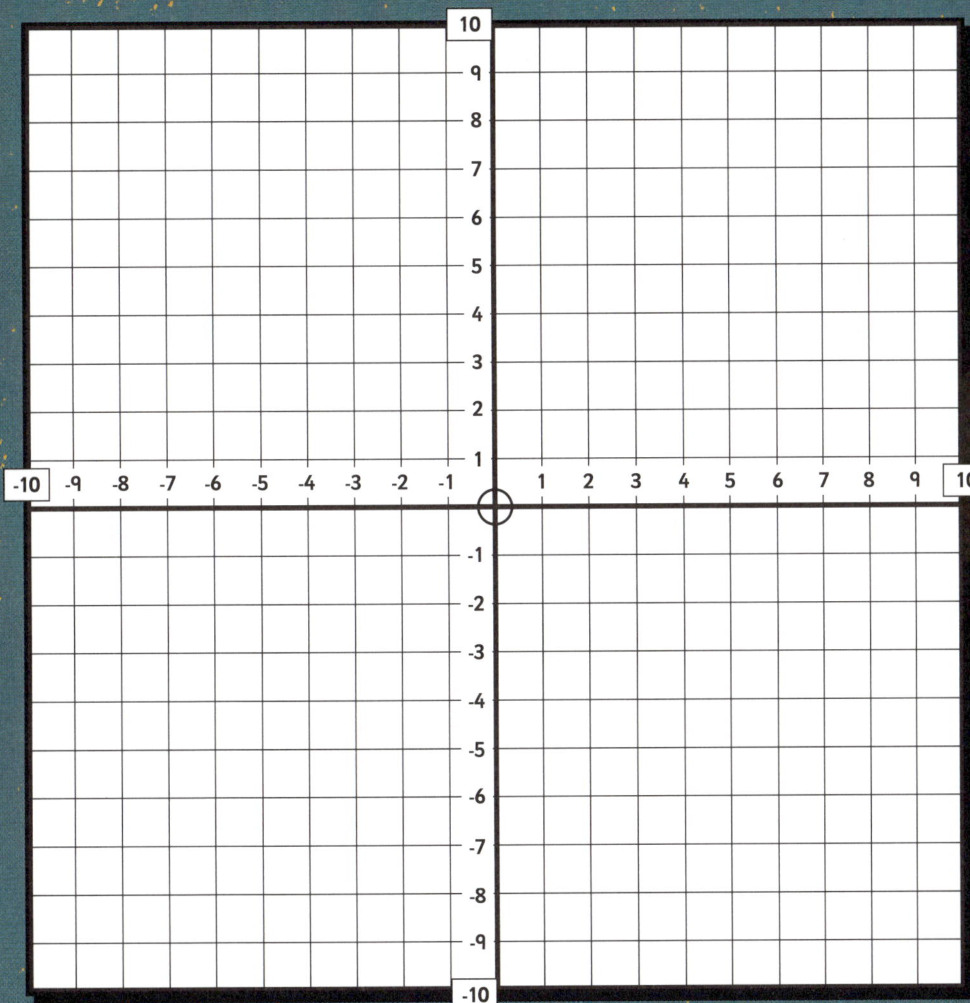

1

Look at the coordinates of where each tool is. Follow the instructions that show where Gromit moved the tool to and write down the new coordinates.

a. Spanner - start at (5, 4)	← **6**	↓ **6**	← **2**	→ **5**	
b. Hammer - start at (-6, -5)	→ **8**	↑ **8**	← **2**	↑ **1**	
c. Screwdriver - start at (-8, 8)	↓ **4**	→ **4**	↓ **4**	→ **4**	
d. Tape measure - start at (7, -3)	→ **1**	↑ **6**	↓ **8**	← **4**	
e. Drill - start at (-9, -9)	→ **3**	→ **3**	→ **3**	↑ **7**	
f. Pliers - start at (1, -1)	← **9**	↑ **4**	→ **5**	↓ **7**	

LINE GRAPHS

1

Wallace is testing a new tea-making machine and records how the water temperature changes over time. Gromit suggests plotting the data on a line graph.

a. How many minutes does it take for the water to reach 85°C?

b. How much does the temperature increase between 2 minutes and 8 minutes?

c. Does the water heat up at a consistent rate throughout the 10 minutes?

d. Between which two consecutive minutes does the largest temperature increase occur?

2

Wallace and Gromit are testing two different kettles for their tea. Gromit uses the old electric kettle, while Wallace tests a new, faster model. They record how the water temperature changes over time for both kettles to see which heats faster.

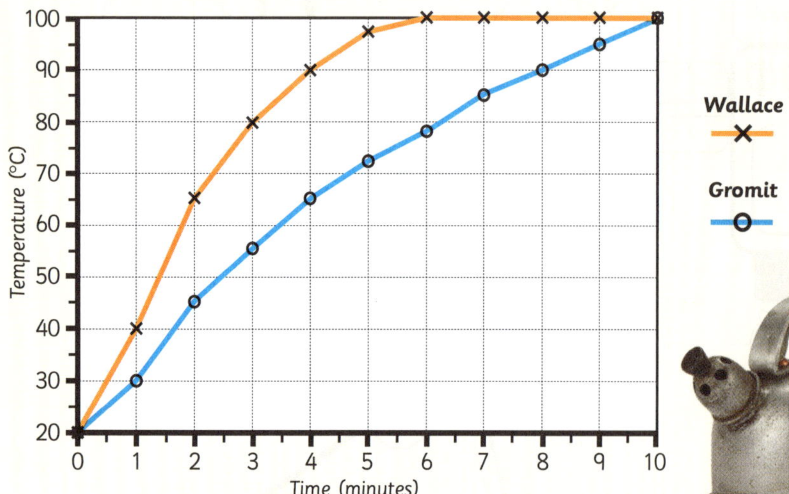

Time (minutes)	Gromit's Kettle (°C)	Wallace's Kettle (°C)
0	20	20
1	30	40
2	45	65
3	55	80
4	65	90
5	72	98
6	78	100
7	85	100
8	90	100
9	95	100
10	98	100

a. Which kettle heats water faster?

b. At 5 minutes, which kettle is hotter, and by how much?

c. How many minutes after Wallace's kettle reaches 90°C does Gromit's kettle reach the same temperature?

d. For how many minutes does Wallace's kettle remain at 100°C before Gromit's kettle reaches 98°C?

e. Between 3 and 5 minutes, which kettle shows the greatest increase in temperature, and by how much?

TIMETABLES

Wendolene has a busy week running her wool shop and ensures every task is scheduled to the minute. Her timetable includes six key tasks, with unique start and end times, for each day from Monday to Saturday.

1

Look at Wendolene's timetable and answer the questions.

	Monday	Tuesday	Wednesday	Thursday	Friday	Saturday
Open shop & organise	08:57 09:22	08:54 09:18	08:59 09:26	08:58 09:19	08:56 09:20	08:43 09:12
Customer orders	09:22 10:47	09:18 10:41	09:26 10:55	09:19 10:42	09:20 10:46	09:12 10:53
Wool delivery	10:47 11:12	10:41 11:06	10:55 11:20	10:42 11:07	10:46 11:11	10:53 11:17
Tea break with Preston	11:12 11:37	11:06 11:31	11:20 12:43	11:07 11:32	11:11 11:36	11:17 11:40
Pack & send orders	11:37 12:43	11:31 12:39	11:43 12:48	11:32 12:40	11:36 12:44	11:40 12:57
Inventory check & clean	16:18 17:03	15:42 16:29	16:14 16:59	15:39 16:24	16:13 16:56	15:47 16:32

a. On which day does Wendolene start her tasks the earliest?

b. How long does Wendolene spend on customer orders on Wednesday?

c. Which task is scheduled for the longest duration on Friday?

d. How many minutes does Wendolene spend on tea breaks with Preston on Monday?

e. Which task does Wendolene finish the latest during the week?

f. How much longer is the 'Pack and send orders' task on Saturday compared to Thursday?

2

Before starting work each day, Wendolene decides to spend 25 minutes having a cup of tea and a slice of toast immediately before opening the shop. Complete the timetable.

	Monday	Tuesday	Wednesday	Thursday	Friday	Saturday
Cup of tea & toast						
Open shop & organise	08:57 09:22	08:54 09:18	08:59 09:26	08:58 09:19	08:56 09:20	08:43 09:12

TIMETABLES

Gromit plans his week carefully to balance relaxation and work. He creates a timetable to organise his tasks and ensure he still has time for a relaxing tea break each afternoon.

1

Answer these question about Gromit's timetable.

	Monday	Tuesday	Wednesday	Thursday	Friday	Saturday	Sunday
Gardening	09:03 – 10:28			08:07 – 09:32			
Reading	11:11 – 12:07			10:13 – 11:26			
Fixing garden tools		08:26 – 09:54					
Knitting socks		11:08 – 12:21					09:02 – 10:31
Grocery shopping			09:35 – 10:22				
Baking scones			11:02 – 11:58				
Visiting library						10:07 – 11:21	
Listening to music						13:12 – 14:38	
Taking a walk							11:14 – 12:27
Tea with Wallace	15:29 – 16:02	16:03 – 16:34	15:06 – 15:35	16:11 – 16:41	15:27 – 16:00	15:30 – 16:01	16:05 – 16:37

a. How long does Gromit's tea break with Wallace last on Wednesday compared to Monday?

b. Gromit gardens twice in the week. How long does he garden for on each of the days?

c. How long does Gromit spend knitting socks on each day?

d. What is the difference in time spent grocery shopping on Wednesday versus baking scones on the same day?

e. What is the total amount of time Gromit spends listening to music during the week?

f. What is Gromit's earliest starting task during the week?

2

Look at the table and work out how long Gromit spends on activities each day.

	Monday	Tuesday	Wednesday	Thursday	Friday	Saturday	Sunday
Total time spent on activities							

PIE CHARTS

Feathers McGraw is organising his secret stash of stolen jewels. He wants to split them by type - diamonds, rubies, emeralds and sapphires. He creates a pie chart to show the proportions.

1

Answer the questions about what types of jewels Feathers stole.

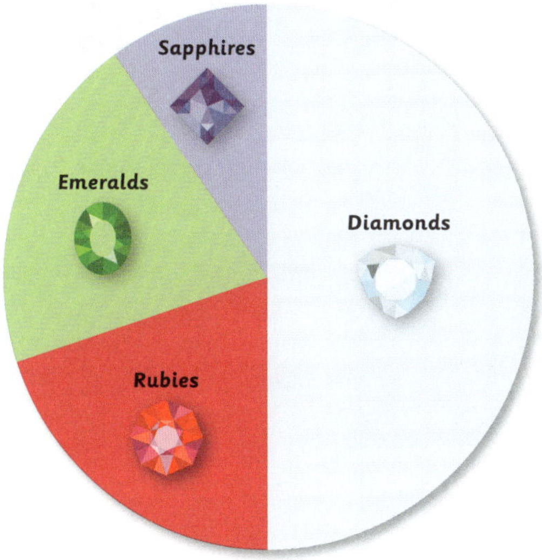

TOTAL NUMBER OF JEWELS IS 80

a. How many are diamonds?

b. Feathers has the same amount of which two types of jewel?

c. 10% of the jewels are sapphires. How many is that?

d. How many jewels are rubies?

2

Answer the questions about where Feathers stole the jewels from.

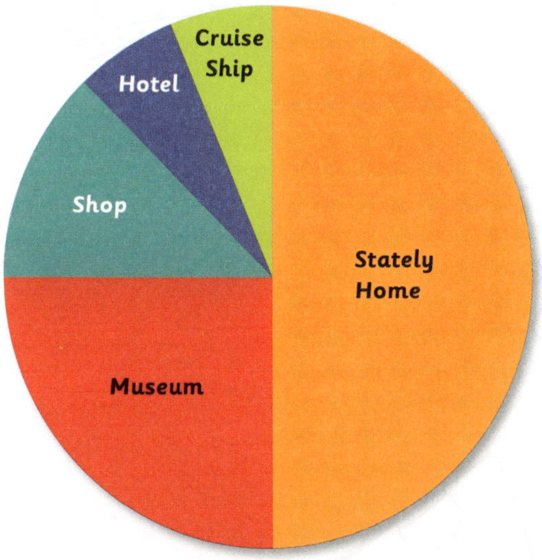

TOTAL NUMBER OF JEWELS IS 80

a. Where were most of the jewels stolen from?

b. How many jewels were stolen from a stately home?

c. What percentage of jewels were stolen from a museum?

d. How many jewels were stolen from a museum?

ANSWERS

Page 2

1. a. 8,675,403 b. 3,192,784 c. 9,048,265 d. 6,431,900
2. a. 1,420,312 b. 2,450,450 c. 3,830,678 d. 4,540,890 e. 5,860,123
3. a. 7,385,210 b. 7,245,210 c. 3 (hundred thousand) d. 7,645,210 e. 6,845,210

Page 3

1. a. 384,400 b. 384,400 c. 384,000 d. 380,000 e. 400,000
2. a. 50,000 b. 89,000 c. 23,700 d. 12,350 e. 100,000
3. a. 20,000 b. 93,000 c. 42,600 d. 11,130 e. 100,000

Page 4

1. a. 6 b. 5,000,000 c. 23 hundred thousands d. 6,000,000 e. 5 (hundred thousand) f. 2,000,000 g. 3 h. 4,600,000

Page 5

1. a. -9°C b. -3°C c. -16°C d. 2°C e. -13°C f. -5°C g. -25°C h. 2°C i. -35°C j. -9°C
2. a. -10,-5,**0**,5,**10**,15
   b. 20,15,10,**5**,0,**-5**
   c. **-15**,-12,-9,**-6**,-3,0
   d. 5,1,**-3**,-7,**-11**,-15
   e. 13,7,**1**,-5,**-11**,-17
3. a. -13°C b. 4°C c. -25°C d. -4°C e. -5°C

Page 6

1. CXCIV = 194, CCCXLV = 345, DCXVI = 616, DCCLIX = 759, CDLXXXII = 482, CMXCIX = 999
2. a. 348 - CCCXLVIII
   - Three hundred forty-eight

   b. 792 - DCCXCII
   - Seven hundred ninety-two

   c. 944 - CMXLIV
   - Nine hundred forty-four

   d. 476 - CDLXXVI
   - Four hundred seventy-six

   e. 831 - DCCCXXXI
   - Eight hundred thirty-one
3. a. XCIX, CCC, CDL, M = 99, 300, 450, 1000
   b. IV, LX, DCC, CM = 4, 60, 700, 900
   c. IX, CCCLX, D, DCXIV = 9, 360, 500, 614
   d. LXXX, CXLIV, DCXL, M = 80, 144, 640, 1000
   e. XIX, CDXXII, DCCC, CMXC = 19, 422, 800, 990

Page 7

1. a. 6,903 b. 7,987 c. 7,501 d. 8,183
2. a. 6845 + 2376 = 9,221
   b. 7293 + 1847 = 9,140
   c. 5634 + 2498 = 8,132
   d. 8421 + 1352 = 9,773
3. row 5. 2,314, 3,528, 4,197, 2,489, 3,162
   row 4. 5,842, 7,725, 6,686, 5,651
   row 3. 13,567, 14,411, 12,337
   row 2. 27,978, 26,748
   row 1. 54,726

Page 8

1. a. 7,825 – 4,639 = 3,186
   b. 6,904 – 2,758 = 4,146
   c. 8,316 – 3,427 = 4,889
   d. 9,742 – 5,856 = 3,886
2. Questions B and D are correct and should have a tick.
3. a. 7,834 – 4,678 = 3,156
   b. 9,206 – 2,749 = 6,457
   c. 8,592 – 3,758 = 4,834
   d. 6,731 – 4,582 = 2,149

Page 9

1. a. 800 + 600 = 1,400
   b. 1,100 + 800 = 1,900
   c. 4,000 + 9,000 = 13,000
   d. 100,000 + 80,000 = 180,000
2. a. 45 + 35 = 80, 450 + 350 = 800, 450 + 356 = 806
   b. 38 + 27 = 65, 380 + 270 = 650, 388 + 270 = 658
   c. 29 + 34 = 63, 290 + 340 = 630, 301 + 340 = 641
   d. 47 + 31 = 78, 4,700 + 3,100 = 7,800, 4,700 + 3,900 = 8,600
   e. 23 + 67 = 90, 230,000 + 670,000 = 900,000, 230,000 + 700,000 = 930,000
3. a. 156 + 189 = 345
   b. 243 + 176 = 419
   c. 389 + 212 = 601
   d. 317 + 284 = 601
   e. 145 + 236 = 381

Page 10

1. a. 764 - 528 = 236
   b. 892 - 457 = 435
   c. 675 - 389 = 286
   d. 947 - 614 = 333
   e. 803 - 476 = 327
2. a. 415 b. 326 c. 317 d. 258 e. 274 f. 382
3. a. 784 - 329 = 455
   b. 652 - 178 = 474
   c. 915 - 436 = 479
   d. 704 - 245 = 459
   e. 568 - 132 = 436

Page 11

1. a. 2,345 + 1,876 + 738 = 4,959
   b. 4,562 - 2,319 - 738 = 1,505
   c. 127 - 84 + 45 = 88
   d. 1,924 - 1,678 + 345 = 591
   e. 234 - 96 = 138

Page 12

1. Prime numbers that should be circled are: 5, 11, 13, 17, 29, 31, 37
2. Prime Only = 2
   Prime and Odd = 5, 13, 23, 31
   Odd = 9, 15, 21, 35
3. Prime Numbers = 31, 37, 41, 43, 47, 53, 59, 61, 67, 71, 73, 79

   Square Numbers = 36, 49 and 64

Page 13

1. a. 137 × 3 = 411
   b. 214 × 4 = 856
   c. 326 × 7 = 2,282
   d. 451 × 8 = 3,608
2. a. 132 × 4 = 528
   b. 246 × 3 = 738
   c. 527 × 6 = 3,162
   d. 684 × 9 = 6,156
3. a. 1,234 × 3 = 3,702
   b. 2,145 × 4 = 8,580
   c. 3,206 × 2 = 6,412
   d. 1,412 × 5 = 7,060
   e. 1,567 × 6 = 9,402
   f. 2,438 × 3 = 7,314

Page 14

1. a. $12 \times 34 = 408$
b. $23 \times 41 = 943$
c. $21 \times 32 = 672$

2. a. $44 \times 22 = 968$
b. $34 \times 21 = 714$
c. $41 \times 21 = 861$
d. $33 \times 23 = 759$

3. a. $73 \times 26 = 1,898$
b. $58 \times 32 = 1,856$
c. $63 \times 46 = 2,898$

Page 15

1. a. $245 \div 6 = 40$ r5
b. $374 \div 8 = 46$ r6
c. $563 \div 9 = 62$ r5
d. $1,456 \div 7 = 208$
e. $2,312 \div 5 = 462$ r2
f. $3,827 \div 6 = 637$ r5

2. a. $1,245 \div 5 = 249$
$< 9,876 \div 9 = 1,097$ r3

b. $3,612 \div 6 = 602 =$
$= 4,214 \div 7 = 602$

c. $2,734 \div 4 = 683$ r2
$> 1,248 \div 6 = 208$

d. $4,567 \div 7 = 652$ r3
$< 5,672 \div 8 = 709$

e. $3,896 \div 8 = 487$
$> 1,482 \div 5 = 296$ r2

Page 16

1. a. $1,248 \div 12 = 104$
b. $2,736 \div 12 = 228$
c. $3,452 \div 12 = 287$ r8
d. $4,915 \div 12 = 409$ r7

Page 17

1. a. $1,236 \times 12 = 14,832$
b. $2,142 \div 18 = 119$
c. $1,024 \times 12 = 12,288$
d. $2,438 \div 34 = 71$ r24
so he will need 72 trucks.
e. $1,572 \div 9 = 174$ r6

Page 18

1. a. $1\frac{1}{2} = \frac{3}{2}$ b. $2\frac{3}{4} = \frac{11}{4}$
c. $3\frac{2}{5} = \frac{17}{5}$ d. $4\frac{4}{7} = \frac{32}{7}$
e. $5\frac{3}{6} = \frac{33}{6}$

2. a. $1\frac{3}{8} = \frac{11}{8}$ b. $2\frac{5}{6} = \frac{17}{6}$
c. $3\frac{4}{9} = \frac{31}{9}$

3. a. $\frac{9}{4} = 2\frac{1}{4}$ b. $\frac{14}{5} = 2\frac{4}{5}$
c. $\frac{19}{6} = 3\frac{1}{6}$

Page 19

1. a. $2\frac{1}{8} + 1\frac{3}{8} = 3\frac{4}{8} = 3\frac{1}{2}$
b. $5\frac{4}{10} - 2\frac{3}{10} = 3\frac{1}{10}$
c. $4\frac{5}{12} + 1\frac{3}{12} = 5\frac{8}{12} = 5\frac{2}{3}$
d. $6\frac{7}{14} - 3\frac{4}{14} = 3\frac{3}{14}$
e. $7\frac{2}{6} + 2\frac{1}{6} = 9\frac{3}{6} = 9\frac{1}{2}$

2.
a. $2\frac{1}{4} + 1\frac{2}{8} = 2\frac{2}{8} + 1\frac{2}{8} = 3\frac{4}{8} = 3\frac{1}{2}$
b. $4\frac{3}{5} - 2\frac{1}{10} = 4\frac{6}{10} - 2\frac{1}{10} = 2\frac{5}{10} = 2\frac{1}{2}$
c. $3\frac{1}{6} + 1\frac{2}{3} = 3\frac{1}{6} + 1\frac{4}{6} = 4\frac{5}{6}$
d. $5\frac{5}{12} - 2\frac{1}{6} = 5\frac{5}{12} - 2\frac{2}{12} = 3\frac{3}{12} = 3\frac{1}{4}$
e. $6\frac{3}{8} + 1\frac{5}{16} = 6\frac{6}{16} + 1\frac{5}{16} = 7\frac{11}{16}$
f. $3\frac{7}{9} + 1\frac{4}{18} = 3\frac{14}{18} - 1\frac{4}{18} = 2\frac{10}{18} = 2\frac{5}{9}$

3. a. $3\frac{1}{2}$ b. $2\frac{1}{2}$ c. $1\frac{9}{10}$

Page 20

1. a. $\frac{10}{8} + \frac{17}{16} = \frac{20}{16} + \frac{17}{16} = \frac{37}{16}$
b. $\frac{9}{4} - \frac{9}{8} = \frac{18}{8} - \frac{9}{8} = \frac{9}{8}$
c. $\frac{10}{6} + \frac{13}{12} = \frac{20}{12} + \frac{13}{12} = \frac{33}{12}$
d. $\frac{20}{9} - \frac{5}{3} = \frac{20}{9} - \frac{15}{9} = \frac{5}{9}$
e. $\frac{13}{10} + \frac{7}{5} = \frac{13}{10} + \frac{14}{10} = \frac{27}{10}$
f. $\frac{5}{3} - \frac{6}{5} = \frac{25}{15} - \frac{18}{15} = \frac{7}{15}$

2.
a. $\frac{6}{2} - \frac{6}{5} = \frac{30}{10} - \frac{12}{10} = \frac{18}{10} = 1\frac{8}{10} = 1\frac{4}{5}$
b. $\frac{5}{6} + \frac{3}{10} = \frac{25}{30} + \frac{9}{30} = \frac{34}{30} = 1\frac{4}{30} = 1\frac{2}{15}$
c. $\frac{22}{10} - \frac{3}{8} = \frac{88}{40} - \frac{15}{40} = \frac{73}{40} = 1\frac{33}{40}$

Page 21: Multiplying Fractions

1. a. $\frac{1}{3}$ b. $\frac{3}{10}$ c. $\frac{4}{15}$ d. $\frac{1}{5}$

2. a. $\frac{3}{5} \times 6 = \frac{18}{5} = 3\frac{3}{5}$
b. $\frac{1}{2} \times 7 = \frac{7}{2} = 3\frac{1}{2}$
c. $\frac{5}{6} \times 3 = \frac{15}{6} = 2\frac{1}{2}$
d. $\frac{4}{5} \times 8 = \frac{32}{5} = 6\frac{2}{5}$
e. $\frac{2}{3} \times 5 = \frac{10}{3} = 3\frac{1}{3}$

Page 22

1. a. $\frac{3}{4} < \frac{5}{6}$ b. $\frac{7}{12} < \frac{2}{3}$ c. $\frac{4}{9} > \frac{3}{8}$
d. $\frac{5}{12} < \frac{3}{6}$ e. $\frac{7}{10} < \frac{9}{12}$ f. $\frac{8}{11} < \frac{10}{12}$
g. $\frac{6}{8} = \frac{9}{12}$ h. $\frac{5}{6} > \frac{7}{9}$

2. a. $\frac{15}{8}, \frac{46}{8}, \frac{52}{8}, \frac{36}{8}$ $\frac{15}{8}, \frac{18}{4}, \frac{23}{4}, \frac{13}{2}$
b. $\frac{25}{16}, \frac{34}{16}, \frac{84}{16}, \frac{54}{16}$ $\frac{25}{16}, \frac{17}{8}, \frac{27}{8}, \frac{21}{4}$
c. $\frac{50}{20}, \frac{112}{20}, \frac{70}{20}, \frac{56}{20}$ $\frac{50}{20}, \frac{28}{10}, \frac{35}{10}, \frac{28}{5}$

Page 23

1. a. 4 : 3 b. 1 : 2 c. 8 : 4 = 2 : 1
d. 3 : 12 = 1 : 4 e. 2 : 8 = 1 : 4 f. 12 : 1
g. 8 : 3 h. 4 : 2 = 2 : 1 i. 1 : 12

2. Cogs – 5, Screws – 3, Springs – 15,
Pulleys – 4, Bolts – 2, Levers – 1

3. a. 6 : 9 = 2 : 3
b. 8 + 2 : 4 = 10 : 4 = 5 : 2
c. 3 : 5 = 12 : 20 so 20 pulleys

Page 24

1. a. £3 b. £20 c. £50 d. £2 e. £15
f. £10 g. £30 h. £5 i. £7 j. £30
k. £45 l. £10

2. a. 33% of £150 = £49.50
b. 12% of £200 = £24
c. 67% of £300 = £201
d. 18% of £400 = £72
e. 44% of £500 = £220
f. 29% of £600 = £174

3. a. £120 b. £119 c. £110

Page 25

1.

Side	Length	Scale Factor 4	Scale Factor 6	Scale Factor 10
a	5cm	20cm	30cm	50cm
b	6cm	24cm	36cm	60cm
c	3.5cm	14cm	21cm	35cm
d	9cm	36cm	54cm	90cm
e	2cm	8cm	12cm	20cm
f	7.5cm	30cm	45cm	75cm

2.

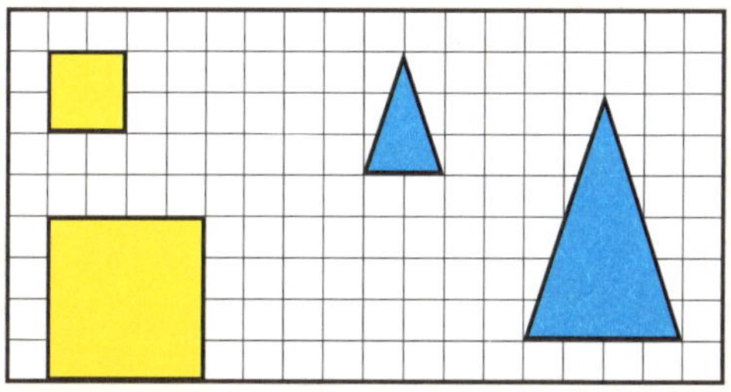

Page 26

1.

	x	3x	2x + 4	5x - 5
a	1	3	6	0
b	4	12	12	15
c	6	18	16	25
d	10	30	24	45
e	11	33	26	50

2.

	X = 8	C = 3	4X - 3C =	32 - 9 =	23
a.	X = 4	C = 5	3X + 2C =	12 + 10 =	22
b.	X = 3	C = 2	5X - 6C	15 - 12 =	3
c.	X = 10	C = 12	2X - C + 5 =	20 - 12 + 5 =	13
d.	X = 5	C = 3	$\frac{20}{x}$ + 2C =	4 + 6 =	10
e.	X = 15	C = 4	$\frac{60}{x}$ + 5C - 10 =	4 + 20 - 10 =	14

3. a. 1 b. 1 c. 12 d. 14 e. 24

Page 27

1.

	$2x + 3$	$5x - 3x$	$3x + 5 - x$	$5x + 11$	$6x + 3x + 2$
$x=1$	5	2	7	16	11
$x=2$	7	4	9	21	20
$x=3$	9	6	11	26	29
$x=5$	13	10	15	36	47
$x=10$	23	20	25	61	92
$x=20$	43	40	45	111	182
$x=50$	103	100	105	261	452
$x=61$	125	122	127	316	551
$x=73$	149	146	151	376	659
$x=99$	201	198	203	506	893

Page 28

1. a. 17 wedges b. 15 cogs
c. 5, 8, 11 pies d. 56 pounds
e. 112 tasks in 7 days f. 132cm
g. 65 flowers after 5 months

Page 29

1. a. < b. = c. > d. < e. <
f. > g. > h. > i. = j. <

2. a. 120cm, 15,000mm, 1200m, 1.5 km
b. 400g, 0.6kg, 0.8kg, 1.2kg
c. 850ml, 1.2 litres, 3.2 litres, 3500ml
d. 250cm, 3.5m, 4500mm, 0.45km
e. 5g, 0.007kg, 0.2kg, 2kg

3. a. 250mm b. 80cm c. 3.5m

Page 30

1. a. 16m b. 22m c. 20m
d. 24m e. 20m f. 22m

2. a. 44m b. 34m c. 46m

Page 31

1. a. $16m^2$ b. $10m^2$ c. $12m^2$
d. $11m^2$ e. $12m^2$ f. $12m^2$

2. a. $8m^2$ b. $4.5m^2$ c. $8m^2$

3. a. $5m^2$ b. $14m^2$ c. $32m^2$

Page 32

Furniture		Area
Table	0.8 x 1.8	$1.44m^2$
Chair	0.4 x 0.6	$0.24m^2$
Sofa	0.6 x 1.6	$0.96m^2$
Bookcase	$\frac{1.0 \times 1.0}{2}$	$0.5m^2$
Cupboard	0.6 x 0.6	$0.36m^2$
Desk	0.18 + 0.18 + 0.36	$0.72m^2$
Fridge	0.36 + 0.04	$0.40m^2$
Rug	0.32 + 0.32	$0.64m^2$
Cooker	0.36 + 0.16 + 0.36	$0.88m^2$
Television Stand	0.32 + 0.02 + 0.02	$0.36m^2$

Page 33

1. a. 6.25 miles = 10.0km
b. 1.75 miles = 2.8km
c. 0.25 mile = 0.4km
d. 3.5 miles = 5.6km
e. 4.75 miles = 7.6km
f. 2.5 miles = 4.0km
g. 7 miles = 11.2km
h. 5.5 miles = 8.8km
i. 8.25 miles = 13.2km
j. 1.5 miles = 2.4km

2. a. 5km > 3 miles b. 10km > 6.2 miles
c. 8km = 5 miles d. 2km < 1.5 miles
e. 15km > 9 miles, f. 12km = 7.5 miles
g. 20km > 12 miles h. 3km < 1.9 miles
i. 7km < 4.5 miles, j. 25km > 15.5 miles

3. a. No, the parlour is exactly 5 miles away.
b. No, the park is exactly 3 miles away
c. 8 miles.

Page 34

1. a. acute b. reflex, c. right d. acute, e. obtuse
f. obtuse, g. reflex, h. acute i. right

Page 35

1. a. 100° b. 165° c. 80° d. 270° e. 15°

2. a. 90° b. 90° c. 60° d. 108° e. 120° f. 135°

Page 36

1. a. 96° b. 65° c. 211° d. 153° e. 76° f. 160°

2. a. $x = 44°, y = 136°, z = 44°$
b. $x = 71°, y = 109°, z = 71°$
c. $x = 19°, y = 161°, z = 19°$
d. $x = 59°, y = 121°, z = 59°$

Page 37

1. a. 60° b. 30° c. 20°

2. The correctly labelled shapes are **a**, **d** and **e**.

Page 38

1. a.

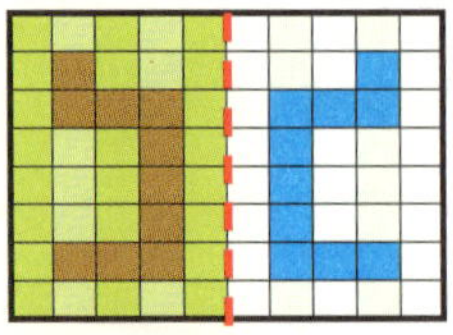

b.

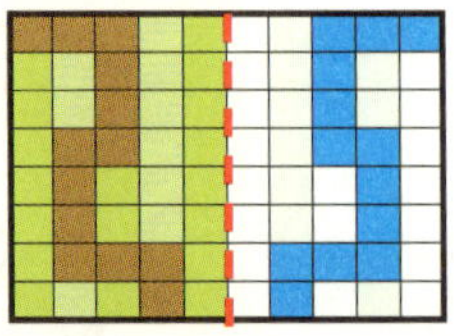

c.

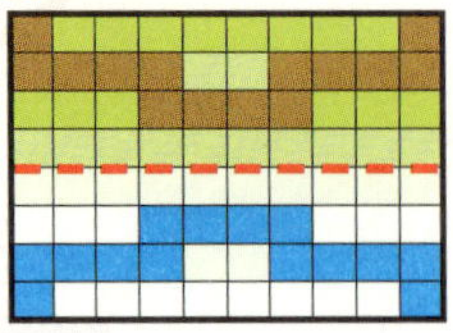

d.

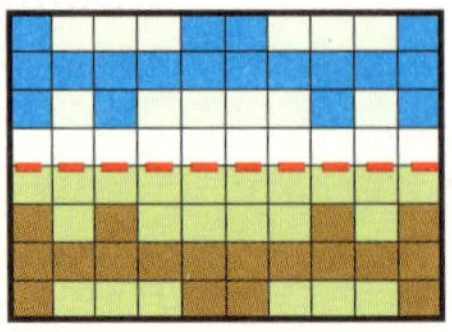

2.

Page 39

1. a. right: 5, up: 4 b. left: 3, down: 3
c. down: 6, right: 5 d. down: 6, right: 4
e. right: 4, up: 2 f. down: 3, left: 5

2.

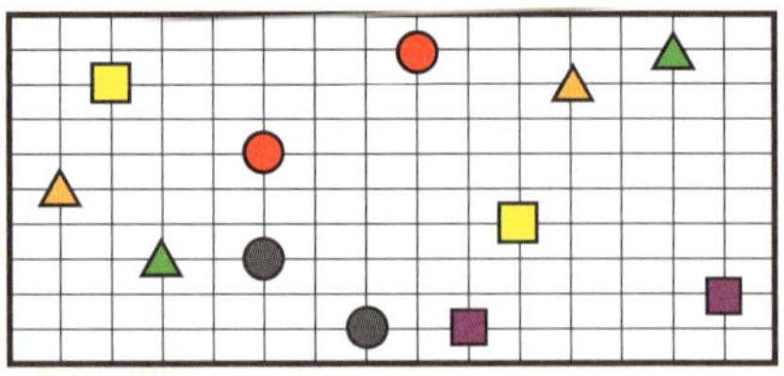

Page 40

1. a.  b.  c. 
d.  e.  f. 

Page 41

1. a. (2, -2) b. (0, 4) c. (0, 0)
d. (4, -5) e. (0, -2) f. (-3, -4)

Page 42

1. a. 7 minutes b. 45 degrees c. No, the heating rate slows down after 7 minutes, as the temperature changes less steeply on the graph between 7 and 10 minutes d. the largest temperature increase occurs between 1 minute (30°C) and 2 minutes (45°C)

2. a. Wallace's kettle b. Wallace's kettle by 26 °C
c. 4 minutes d. 4 minutes e. Wallace's kettle shows the greatest increase, by 18°C

Page 43

1. a. Saturday b. 1hour 29 minutes c. Customer orders
d. 25 minutes e. Wendolene finishes "Inventory check and clean" the latest on Monday at 17:03
f. The task is 9 minutes longer on Saturday

2.

	Monday	Tuesday	Wednesday	Thursday	Friday	Saturday
Cup of tea & toast	08:32	08:29	08:34	08:33	08:31	08:18
	08:57	08:54	08:59	08:58	08:56	08:43
Open shop & organise	08:57	08:54	08:59	08:58	08:56	08:43
	09:22	09:18	09:26	09:19	09:20	09:12

Page 44

1. a. Gromit's tea break lasts 33 mins on Monday and 29 mins on Wednesday b. 1hr 25 mins
c. 1hr 13 mins on Tuesday and 1hr 29 mins on Sunday
d. 9 mins e. 1hr 26 mins
f. Gardening on Thursday beginning at 08:07

2.

	Monday	Tuesday	Wednesday	Thursday	Friday	Saturday	Sunday
Total time spent on activities	85mins + 56mins + 33mins = **174mins or 2 hours 54 mins**	88mins + 73mins + 31mins = **192mins or 3 hours 12 mins**	47mins + 56mins + 29mins = **132mins or 2 hours 12 mins**	85mins + 73mins + 30mins = **188mins or 3 hours 8 mins**	**33 mins**	74mins + 86mins + 31mins = **191mins or 3 hours 11 mins**	73mins + 89mins + 32mins = **194mins or 3 hours 14 mins**

Page 45

1. a. 40 b. rubies and emeralds c. 8 d. 16

2. a. Stately Home b. 40 c. 25% d. 20